# Recipes of love

MARIKA MITSOTAKI

# Recipes of love

Foreword:
ALEXANDRA MITSOTAKI

Text:
EMMANUELA NIKOLAIDOU

Recipes edited by:
KATERINA MITSOTAKI

Translated by:
MARIA ADAMANTIDIS COUTROUBAKI

**KERKYRA**
p u b l i c a t i o n s

ATHENS 2012

© *Marika Mitsotaki, Alexandra Mitsotaki, Katerina Mitsotaki*
*Original title in Greek:* Μαρίκα Μητσοτάκη: Συνταγές με... ιστορία
Published by the LIVANI PUBLISHING ORGANIZATION S.A., 2011

*ISBN: 978-960-9490-18-4*
© *Kerkyra Publications SA – Economia Publishing*
*1st English edition, November 2012*

*Series:* Modern Greek Culture

*Author:* MARIKA MITSOTAKI
*Text:* EMMANUELA NIKOLAIDOU
*Recipes edited by:* KATERINA MITSOTAKI
*Translated by:* MARIA ADAMANTIDIS COUTROUBAKI

*Food photographer:* MICHAEL KOUVIDIS
*Family photographs:* VASSILIKI GEORGIOU – FOCUS ART,
   GIORGOS PAPADAKIS – PAPADAKISPRESS,
   PERSONAL ARCHIVE (UNPUBLISHED MATERIAL),
   ARCHIVE OF THE MITSOTAKIS FOUNDATION
*Backcover photograph:* STUDIO PATRIDIS

**Production: Kerkyra Publications – Economia Publishing**
Publication Coordinator: Efi Andrikopoulou
Layout: Makis Christopoulos, Atelier Kerkyra

Distribution

KERKYRA Publications S.A.
6-8 Vlahava street, 105 51 Athens-Greece
Tel.: 0030-210-3314.714, Fax: 0030-210-3252.283

**www.economia.gr, sales@economia.gr**

# Contents

## Recipes – Savory dishes

**Recipes – Sweets**

# Foreword

This book is a gift –a gift I wanted to make to my mother. When the Greek version came out on November 29, 2011, the day of her 81st birthday, she was deeply moved and profoundly happy. She had had a difficult year spending months in hospital and rehabilitation. The "book of her recipes", which in the end was to become also the book of her life, was actually designed to help her over those long months. Help her to regain her spirit, her joie-de-vivre and the strength to wage yet another battle for her health. It provided her with something to look forward to. Working on it allowed her to talk about food, to pick recipes, to taste and to think about cooking even when she could not stand in her kitchen any more. Just as importantly, it helped her reminisce and unfold memories of her childhood years, of her love for our father, of the joys and sorrows of family life. As a mother of four, a grandmother of thirteen and a great-grandmother of five, she had had plenty.

That autumn day in Athens, when the book was publicly launched, was her day. She was acknowledged and recognized not as the wife of my father –a prominent politician– but in her own right. That day she was the center of everybody's attention, admiration and love. She deserved it and I am glad my sister Katerina –who worked on the recipes– and I speeded up the process of finishing the book because, as it turned out, it was to be her last public appearance. She left us a few months later.

Her life certainly informed her cooking: there was pre-war Athens, my grandmother's recipes and the support, as it were, of American technology –meaning the refrigerator and the blender– which she discovered before they became staples of every Greek household; there was the influence of French cuisine during the years of political exile in Paris; and finally, the flavors of Greece and most specially of Crete, her adopted home.

In our family, as in most Greek families, food plays a central role. In fact, there are two things we consistently do at home when we are all together: we eat and we talk! And strangely enough, even while eating, we talk about… food. Food is, in the end, a strong social link: When we are all together, somebody is bound to ask what we are having for dinner. For my mother, the long distance call –almost a daily habit– would inevitably include the question "What's on the menu today?", whereas her welcome from a night out would conclude with, "And how was the food?", just as the return from a long trip abroad was always met with "Did you eat well there, my dear?". But the most important question of all, which made us all feel loved and welcome, remained: "What do you want me to cook for you today?".

Actually the Greek language reflects that reality. In Greek the word for companionship –"syntrofikotita"– combines the prefix "syn", which implies togetherness, with "trofi": "food".

All of us, children and grandchildren, had been asking my mother for years to make this book of family recipes. She agreed but, as it happened, there were always more pressing matters that required her attention. Life has a way of imposing its own rhythm and never allowed her enough free time to turn her attention to this book. Perhaps because, in the end, she was not really interested; for my mother, cooking and eating were part of her daily routine with my father, with us, with her friends –and how do you turn all this into a book? Perhaps she also felt she needed to save her energy and time –both no longer in abundance– in order to cope with real life, which had not always been easy for her.

So, in the end, "the book" became a gift, a gift my sister Katerina and I made to her. But now, as so often happens in life with giving, we have come to realize that this is also a gift we made to ourselves, our children and grandchildren and to the people who have known and loved her. It will keep her recipes alive, not only those related to food and eating but also the one on how to keep a family close together –a recipe for love and fulfillment. And if any proof is needed, one need only glance at the photograph on the back cover of this book, where she looks so astonishingly beautiful and happy.

That is how we choose to remember her.

Alexandra Mitsotaki
November 2012

# Around the table

A glass raised to toast somebody, the smell of cooked food emanating from the pot, the opportunity to discuss the day's latest developments and to make fun of less serious happenings, decisions that need to be taken concerning the family…

The act of gathering around the family table is a ritual of cardinal value, notwithstanding other lifestyle models promoted nowadays. For Kostas and Marika Mitsotaki, these gatherings –a practice which they've followed religiously– unfolded in tandem with a daily routine that was all but commonplace –their family history is closely related to the history of Greece in the years following the Second World War.

The particular moments and events that shaped it are transformed here into the aromas and flavors of a cooking style, recounting those little stories that are usually nestled inside bigger ones…These are tales of family meals told in the style of Marika Mitsotaki who made sure the table was always set, ready to receive the family and keep it together.

• A table laid for lunch or dinner will always be the ideal setup for family get-togethers

"We grew up during the war and the German occupation," she says beginning her account, "and this is why we knew that food is a valuable commodity, one that was terribly scarce during those difficult times, when people were dying in the streets from starvation. Since much earlier times, the art of cooking had been intertwined with the art of hospitality –hospitality in its pure sense of attending to the other's needs, of guaranteeing the availability of the proverbial daily bread and in making sure that no one and nothing is missing, if possible, from the table. This is the way my generation was brought up. True, in the process we also learned how to prepare fine meals, but this was not achieved in the spirit of competition but as part of the effort to cater to the needs of the family and our loved ones.

"This was true for all Greek homes, regardless of their financial situation. And that is exactly why we make it a point to keep to the ritual of the family lunch or dinner, even today, because it gives us the opportunity, or rather, the joy of being together. Ever since Kostas and I got married, we held to the principle of family members lunching together every day, which I believe helped keep the family connected. We tried keeping this daily routine without exception, even in those times when my husband had a terribly full schedule."

So perhaps that explains why Alexandra Mitsotaki, who is present in our conversation, admits that it is well nigh impossible for her to sit and dine by herself.

"It bothers me too, I need the company of people when I'm eating," adds her mother in agreement. "Even today, with the children gone and having their own families, everyone knows that Kostas and I unfailingly lunch at two p.m., and we happily welcome anyone who can join us."

# Grandmother Nonika's kitchen

Marika Yannoukou, subsequently Mitsotaki, was born in the inter-war period to one of the most privileged Athenian families, who –as later events were to prove– was fortunate enough not to have other children. Her maternal grandfather was the well-known industrialist and formidable entrepreneur Zavoyannis. Also involved in politics as a member of parliament for the party that supported Eleftherios Venizelos –the charismatic statesman and builder of modern Greece in the early 20th century– her grandfather represented the district of Piraeus from which he hailed.

When it was time to marry, he chose a sweet and –by all accounts– beautiful young woman from the island of Hydra to be his bride. In her fervor to present him with the much-needed son, she gave birth to twelve girls, of which only four survived into maturity. In the end, following subsequent losses, of this large family and its descendants only one daughter, Marika, was left. As the only remaining child, she was doted upon by her parents and all family relatives and especially her mother's sisters.

Marika Mitsotaki becomes emotional when speaking of her parents.

"They were extraordinary people. My father was a true *bon vivant*, a remarkable man! My mother, Dora, was a terrific homemaker, always making sure that everything was in perfect order… I remember, for instance, that she insisted that I use the pink clothes hanger for my pink dress, the blue one for the blue dress and so on. She was also a fantastic cook and I made a point of watching her in action –I loved to see how she combined ingredients to come up with wonderful flavors… But I also observed what my parents ordered when we travelled, I wanted to know and try new

• Marika Yannoukou, subsequently Mitsotaki, with her father –a true gentleman, by common agreement.

dishes… And that's how I learned to appreciate good food."

Marika greatly loved and admired her mother, naturally, but she had a soft spot for her father –and the feeling was reciprocal. He was an industrious leather merchant of the times and he had a strong emotional bond with his only daughter. By common agreement, he was a true gentleman coming from a financially comfortable family, a hand-some and generous man, forever ready to help people in need. His own mother –Marika's other grandmother– hailed from the island of Andros, and specifically from Batsi, a cosmopolitan village today which was inhabited by Albanian settlers called "Arvanites" in the distant past.

"Kostas teases me," she says laughing, "because to him this explains why I am hard-headed like the proverbially hard-headed "Arvanites" –and, truth be told, he may be right!"

The Yannoukos family home was in one of Athens' first apartment buildings, on 32 Voukourestiou Street, at a time when this pleasant street in the city center was lined with grand villas in luscious gardens. In the first years of their marriage she would set up home with Kostas Mitsotakis in that same building where her parents still resided. Earlier, in her childhood years, her father's greatly successful commercial enterprises combined with her mother's large family fortune would be enough to assure that she would acquire such skills and polish –first class education, foreign languages, dance lessons– that would serve her well in the future…

And it is precisely this same family fortune that would prove a valuable asset in the hard times to come.

"My father-in-law had to shut down his business, during the German occupation," says Kostas Mitsotakis, "but he still had large stocks of leather. At that time, leather was among the most

• At her parents' home on Voukourestiou Street, with early 1950s Athens in the background. The apartment building was one of the few structures standing out among villas and luscious gardens.

important and sought-after commodities. This, combined with the food supplies in the Yannoukos pantry and the overall financial comfort of the family, made it possible for them to survive but also to help many others. For example, Marika's mother would systematically organize free meals for the needy, providing basic foodstuffs. She used to tell us that she would walk everyday from Voukourestiou Street to the Fix brewery to prepare bean soup. She always used to hide a small bottle of cooking oil in her pocket, intending it for the weakest and particularly the children, who needed to take high-calorie meals.

"At that same period," continues Kostas Mitsotakis," I was confined in Athens, together with my brother Haralampos, because Crete was under occupation. For a period of eleven months, I survived on nothing but boiled, oil-less bean soup. I ate no meat, fish, eggs, milk or pasta –nothing but bean soup and perhaps some raisins in summer. Bean soup remains to the day one of my favorite dishes since, paradoxically, I never grew to hate it. I was enrolled in three soup-kitchens: the lawyers' –as I had become a member of the Lawyers Association–, the reserve officers' and the Cretans'. I would go to all three mess halls, one after the other, and consume a plateful of bean soup, using the spoon I always carried in my pocket.

"For the rest of my life, afterwards, I would eat and still do eat everything and, most of all, leafy greens. Often people will send me leafy greens from various places and I'm always happy to have them. The greens of Crete are my favorites, especially the wild growing 'stamnangathi', not the cultivated kind sold in Athens. I also like raw artichokes –they are part of my breakfast when they are in season, cut in pieces, with a little salt and lemon. They make a good accompaniment for wine, too. My children are convinced that I eat too much but it's not true! I'm just a slow eater; I chew every bite twenty or thirty times, even if it's just honey, which is what I start my day with. That said, I like all kinds of food: greens, pulses, fish, chicken, dairy products, cheeses –the lot."

Marika Mitsotaki is also a lover of fine cuisine, which is perfectly normal considering she had a good teacher.

In the words of her childhood friend Virginia "Nita" Eleftheroudaki-Gregou:

"Marika's mother was an amazing cook. She was so good that, as children, whenever we visited for dinner, we would go to the kitchen and lick off any leftovers lining the cooking pots! Our favorite dish was lemon pot roast but, without any doubt, when it came to sweets she had no equal: 'galaktoboureko', Pasta Flora, custard-on-a-plate –all were perfect!"

"For me, the perfect family dessert is the famous marble cake, grandmother Nonika's signature sweet," adds Kyriakos Mitsotakis. It's the classic vanilla-chocolate marble cake, which she executed perfectly every time! I remember that whenever I visited her as a child, there was always a warm, delicious slice waiting for me, just out of the oven. I still believe this was the tastiest cake

I've ever tried. Grandma was an expert cook of sweets, whereas mom is predominantly an expert on savory dishes. Having said that, I must also admit that her 'kourambiedes' are perfect!"

Katerina, the youngest daughter in the Mitsotaki family, still remembers grandmother Nonika's colorful descriptions of her Piraeus paternal home.

"It was," she used to say," a neoclassical villa that stood next to the municipal theater building, with two huge pantries which were always fully stocked, as if she expected to feed an army!"

But she also has memories of her grandmother's house on Voukourestiou Street:

"The kitchen was very large with a marble-topped table in the middle. It was there that grandmother worked and prepared her famous desserts and cookies. There were countless candy bowls in the drawing room, always filled with cookies, biscuits, chocolates, savory sticks etc., prepared for visitors but primarily for her grandchildren whom she would always welcome with her favorite expression: "And what will your choice of a treat be, my little birdie?'

# Adversity and courage

As fate would have it, being an only child turned out to be a fortunate circumstance in the end. And that is because the young "Miss Yannoukou" was to be struck by poliomyelitis, or polio, one of that era's most detested diseases, that left its victims with insurmountable mobility problems.

"My mother had to remain by my side at the New York Presbyterian Hospital for six consecutive months. What would she have done if she had other children to take care of?" she muses.

The disease first manifested itself with a persistent fever.

"I was burning hot for several days," she remembers, "until one morning as I was getting out of bed, I just collapsed. That was only a few days before the 28th of October National Day celebration. I was nine then. It appears I got infected by the germ in the swimming pool and that is why, shortly afterwards, the Americans closed down all swimming pools in Athens to contain the spread of the disease. Up until then there had been only two other cases of polio in Greece –I was the third.

"The situation was very serious. My parents called in a team of medical experts to examine me. Among them was Horemis, the renowned physician who, as he was going out of my room, informed my parents that I would not be able to walk again! Of course I overheard him and understood very well what he meant, even though I was only a child. Right then and there I thought to myself: 'Well, that's what *you* think!'

"Actually, many years afterwards I happened to be seated across Horemis in a meeting. At some point he said: 'Mrs. Mitsotakis, may I ask why you are so aggressive when addressing me?...' 'I am sorry,' I replied, 'I probably did not realize that I was, but I'm afraid it must be because of an old unfinished «business» between us two.' I reminded him of the incident at our house and he was shocked. 'I thank you indeed,' he said in the end. 'I shall include it in my book as an example to be avoided by doctors of the coming generations: they should be very careful of the way they express themselves...'

"Doctors in Greece back then insisted that I would get better with the help of physiotherapy but I was steadily getting worse. It wasn't just the matter of my leg but in the meantime I had also developed scoliosis. The bacterium had affected the entire right-hand side of my spine and, as I was growing up, my body started to take a sideways slant. Back then we used to sew our own clothes and one day, as we were in the process of sewing a skirt, my mother

• As a young girl with her mother aboard the ship taking them to America. The first trip in their effort to defeat a terrible disease is under way.

noticed that one side was shorter than the other. She could not understand why at first, but when she realized that it was not the hemming that was wrong but my spine, she was terribly shocked. In the course of one year, my spine's curve became quite pronounced and the situation got much more serious.

"Meanwhile, there was a war going on and living conditions were far from easy. There were no school buses and no public transport –there was nothing! To go to school, for instance, you either went on foot or you did not go at all! I was attending the Makris Hellenic Schools and I had to walk from my house on Voukourestiou Street to Queen Sophia Avenue, about twenty blocks away. I managed it by putting in a tremendous amount of effort combined with a lot of dogged determination be-cause, actually, my leg was a dead weight, lifeless. But I also had a lot of help from my fellow students, boys and girls. Athens was a small city back then and we all knew each other. They would come by the house, whistle up for me to come down and they would help me walk all the way to the school. They did the same for the way back at noon."

Seeing the curve that was disfiguring her child's back, Marika's mother, who was as determined and persevering as her daughter, declared: "I shall find a way to make my child healthy again!" And so, as soon as the war was over, she contacted her sister who was living in America, married to an award-winning columnist with *The New York Times*. She explained what the problem was and asked them to help bring Marika to the United States, so that she would be examined by the doctors there, because they were more experienced in polio cases. "It was terribly difficult to obtain a visa to visit America in those days and my uncle went all the way to Washington to seek it," Marika Mitsotaki remembers. "In the end, he managed to secure a visa through the intervention of Roosevelt himself, who had a special sensitivity for this matter as he had been struck by the disease himself. That is why he gave us the permit…"

"And then we had to deal with another difficult matter: finding transportation for the trip. After repeated efforts, we managed to secure two tickets aboard a Liberty type ship –they were the first vessels allowed to cross the Atlantic after the war. The passage lasted a full twenty four days, during which my mother slept in the small cabin berth and I used the narrow banquette across it. I still remember our first breakfast on board. A sailor ushered us into the dining area and… lo and behold! The buffet was brimming with toasted-bread sandwiches, muffins, a big slab of butter in the shape of a mountain –just like Lycabettus hill in Athens– fruit jams, sausages –all things we had forgotten existed because of the famine during the war and the German occupation. And truth be told, I was a bit of a gourmand… Aside from this, though, the voyage was long and difficult. I remember that we first stopped in Naples, waiting for the waters to be cleared of naval mines before continuing to Gibraltar. One night, midway through the Atlantic, the ship's sirens sounded. We were terribly scared at first but then we learned it was because Japan had agreed to a cease fire. The sailors celebrated accordingly with lots of liquor and singing… A few days later, we arrived at the Norfolk naval station in Virginia. After meeting up with my aunt and uncle who were waiting for us, we all went to New York.

"We started making the rounds to find the appropriate doctor the next day. Our final choice was a Greek orthopedic doctor from Messinia, professor

• Marika posing with her mother, the children's beloved "Grandma Nonika", who was a wonderful cook and an expert maker of sweets and desserts.

Lantzounis, who lived and worked in the States. This wonderful man gave it his all to help me, almost like a father would for his own child. And as a matter of fact when Kostas and I married we asked him to be our best man! After the first operation, I had to stay for six months in a cast, with my mother constantly at my side. Mind you, by 'in a cast' I mean I had to lay absolutely immobile in bed, on my back, with my eyes looking nowhere but up, towards the ceiling…

"Following this we returned to Greece, where I continued school and then went back to America, alone this time, for the doctors to check my progress. I thought I was done with surgery for good, but there remained a lot of damage that needed fixing. On the very first night, Lantzounis told me: 'Marika, I want to talk to you about a new surgical method. I can try to re-set your spine to an almost perfect straight line, but that would take time and a fair amount of suffering.'

"I was seventeen at the time so I told him 'Let me think about it, but say nothing to my parents yet', as I did not want to have my mother go through another ordeal…

"I left his office and walked all the way from the First to the Sixth Avenue in Manhattan. I was in a daze, crossing the streets without even glancing at traffic lights… The doctor's words were ringing in my ears: 'Marika, you are a young, beautiful woman with your whole life still ahead of you and someday you will fall in love with a handsome fellow… This is worth trying…'

"So I took the decision to undergo surgery for a second time. This was a pioneering procedure which had been tried only on seven other people in America, but I took the risk to go ahead with it and, fortunately, it went very well. Of course, after surgery I told my mother about it and she booked the first flight out and came to New York to help me get through this second difficult phase because, once again, I had to stay in a cast for five months."

This was tough going for a young woman who adored music and dancing and who as a child used to be very good at ballet, but who also never missed a chance to move to the modern beat of the samba, the rumba and yes, tap-dancing! A young woman who, before she had the chance to revel in the joys of youth, was forced to wage protracted battles in hospital rooms and to deal with physical pain as well as with the terrifying possibility of losing her mobility, owing to serious polio-related consequences. And the only reason she emerged victorious from these battles –refuting prognoses that had her unable to walk again– is because she held tight to her great inner courage and strength.

• New York: Marika keeps smiling though wearing a cast, slightly visible under her light, springtime dress.

# Love, Crete and the magnificent red snapper

Marika Mitsotaki was eighteen years old when she returned from the US, her back almost completely straightened.

"One day during the summer holidays –after I had graduated from high school– a friend and I decided to go to Parliament to see what it was all about. Mitsotakis was sitting in one of the front rows and he immediately caught my attention. I asked around about him and was told that he was a promising young MP from Crete, already making a name for himself. At that time Kostas was almost thirty and to be honest, I had my eye on him from the start!"

There was to be another encounter of a certain intensity, as it were, between the pretty Athenian girl and the charming Cretan MP: An usher in Parliament attempted to have Marika exit the elevator to make room for several MPs who were coming in, Mitsotakis among them. The young woman not only refused to exit but gave the young politician her sternest and most intimidating look –even though he had nothing to do with the usher's demand. If anything, she made a lasting impression on him!

"Following these two chance encounters," she remembers, "two years went by before we met again. One evening I put on a pretty dress and went to the gala organized by the Red Cross in honor of Daisy Mavraki who had just won the title of Star Hellas –a rather important event back then! And here was Kostas standing in front of me! As a member of the gala organizing committee, I was on duty serving drinks. So Kostas, tall and handsome, approaches the beverage stand and says:

" 'Whisky on-the-rocks, please.'

" 'For one?' I asked.

" 'No, for two,' he replied, 'one for me and one for you!'

"That was it… We danced and danced and at some point, late in the evening, he says to me:

" 'My friends and I are going to the Athinaia Club –will you join us?'

"So I came up with a good excuse and left my own friends to follow Kostas' group. We danced all night, almost till daybreak."

"We met several times after that but our relationship developed into serious romance in the island of Mykonos. I had gone there with my girl friends and Mitsotakis arrived together with his friend Panos Kokkas on a night of very heavy seas. It was there that our relationship evolved…".

"Mykonos then was nothing like it is today," adds Kostas Mitsotakis. "There were barely two or three small tavernas and if you wanted to make sure that there'd be something for you to eat, you placed an order for lunch or asked to have some food reserved before setting out with the boat for a swim. Otherwise, you just went without lunch!"

"A few months on," Marika continues, "my mother had started to realize that something was afoot, because every now and then bouquets of red roses would be delivered to our house. She had started wondering who they were from."

"And one day she says to my father: 'I'm pretty sure our daughter has a beau but keeps it a secret!'

"'Nonsense!' was my father's reply. 'There is no beau!'

"Mother was not convinced, though, and in order to keep me away from this mysterious stranger, decided to have me spend Christmas with my aunt and uncle in America. I took the news to Kostas and proposed that he came with me but on a different flight, to keep the whole thing under cover. I immediately let my aunt know about my plan, and my uncle as well who, upon meeting Kostas, said:

"'This is a wonderful young gentleman; he will be a very good husband for Marika.'

"To cut a long story short, we were engaged on the day after Christmas, in a Hungarian restaurant that had violin players and a very romantic atmosphere generally!"

• A moment of rest for the young couple in love. Kostas Mitsotakis provides photographic proof of his love for fruit.

"I immediately wrote my parents the news inserting a small photograph of Kostas in the envelope. They were taken completely by surprise. They simply could not figure out 'how on earth she managed to find this guy from Crete' as they kept repeating.

"In the meantime I stayed in America a little longer to buy my trousseau, while Kostas returned to Greece and immediately sent my mother a bouquet of red roses like the ones he had been sending to me. She understood and appreciated his humor and the truth is that my parents grew very fond of him from that moment onwards. Actually, when my father passed away and I had to look into his wallet for his identity card, I found out that he kept a photo of Kostas in there. I was very moved...

"And so we were married in 1953. One of our best men was Lantzounis, my beloved physician, who had made me realize that better health for myself and for my body was something worth fighting for, arguing that one day I would fall in love with a handsome young fellow... As it turned out, he was right!

"Of course, matters were not that easy for me after marriage. I was used to a different lifestyle and was totally unprepared for life with a politician representing a provincial district... Those were difficult years. We had to sail to Crete every weekend, often braving rough seas aboard ageing vessels, and stayed at his parents' home that had no heating and scarcely any hot water.

"One thing that I could barely stand

• Excursions to the countryside –especially in Crete– always culminated in a sumptuous feast.

• The young lovers are all smiles in these snapshots taken on the rare trips away from Kostas Mitsotakis' hectic schedule as a politician on the rise.

was my mother-in-law's cooking. So one day, I walk up to her and brazenly exclaim:

"'Mother, I need to tell you something: your cooking is terrible! You do not use butter or condiments, you do not use mustard or pepper...'

"The only things that she made quite well were the 'kaltsounia'. I had decided to be very direct about how difficult it was for me to accept her cooking, because I wanted us to have a sincere and honest relationship. So, after hearing my complaint, though she was a rather reserved and undemonstrative woman, she waves towards the kitchen and tells me with a great deal of humor:

"'In you go, then, milady!'

"So it was that I started preparing my own dishes and let the others cook their tasteless mush!"

"Our parental home in Crete," explains Kostas Mitsotakis, "was a big house with a wonderful garden but it was old, older than Eleftherios Venizelos' house. My father bought it in 1920 and restored it from the foundations up. We used to call it 'Galaria' and it resembled a military camp as it was always crowded and noisy, teeming with people and children. My mother, sister and brothers and their families –three generations– all lived under this one roof, so there was scarcely any free space left and naturally it was difficult for Marika to adapt at first. But things went smoothly after a little while. She had a problem with the food, yes, but I should add that I made her change some of her habits as well. She learned to eat leafy greens, for instance, and also to use olive oil.

"During the first years of our marriage we used to stay in my parents' house, but for the summer we rented a small house in Akrotiri so we could be by ourselves.

"It was small and rather primitive," remembers Marika, "built on a slope, with a breathtaking view of the port. There was no running water; we had to pull water out of the well! There was a small sitting area and two bedrooms, one for the newly born Dora –or 'Doraki' as we used to call her and, actually, still do– and one for the two of us, also a kitchen and a room for doing the wash. We had three divans and just the basic comforts, but it was freshly painted and clean. I'll never forget the wonderful days we spent there. Besides, we were young and that says it all… We were young and everything was much simpler."

"One day I had gone to the market to shop and the fishmonger tells me:

"'Kyria Marika, are you interested in fresh red snapper?'

"It was truly very fresh, and although I had never prepared fish before, I said 'I'll take it'.

"Upon returning home at around 10 o'clock, I placed the snapper in the pot with just a little leek and nothing else. I didn't even consider adding salt! Then I prepared the mayonnaise in this fantastic American blender that my mother had given me –the famous KitchenAid brand– because she already had one herself. I had the recipe for mayonnaise, which I followed exactly and it came out really tasty. I placed the mayonnaise in the fridge given to us by my father –it was a tremendous luxury to have a fridge in those times– and I let the fish boil alone in the pot, with no other additions. Then, after removing it from the stove, I took Doraki for a swim.

"We came back home at around 1 o'clock and I set the table in the veranda with the panoramic view over the town of Chania.

"Kostas and Doraki sat on the table and I brought out the fish which I had placed on a big serving plate –I was really excited over the thought of serving home-cooked fish, complete with mayonnaise and potatoes on the side! So I first serve Kostas, then myself, and I take my first bite and… oh, what a shock that was! Cooked without any

• The view from the little house in Akrotiri was truly breathtaking. It was from this spot that the infamous red snapper took the plunge to oblivion…

• June 6, 1953: Escorted by her father, beautiful Marika sparkles in her exquisite bridal gown.
• With Dora in her arms, shortly after she was born.
• With firstborn Dora, Alexandra, little Katerina and the famous birthday cake!
• With her three daughters, unwittingly lined up in ascending order… It is the mid-1960s, a little before the coup of the military *junta*.

salt or oil, the fish was absolutely tasteless, it was just not worth eating! To a fledging home-maker like me, this felt like an absolute disaster! 'Come now, calm down, it's not that bad',," said Kostas who was trying to assuage me, 'you will get the recipe next time and you will do it right,' but I would have none of it. 'Don't you see how awful it is?' I replied. 'There will be no next time!'

"Desperate and furious as I was, I grabbed the serving plate –it was part of a beautiful porcelain set– and went up to the edge of the slope. Immediately below was a deep precipice and then, well, the city of Chania… 'Whoosh' went the serving plate, flying into the air and the precipice below –and that was the end of it… Kostas was placating as usual: 'Why on earth did you do that, Marika?' 'Because it was impossible to eat!' I shot back, and so ended, rather ingloriously, the story of the magnificent red snapper!"

Thus, whether in the large house –the "Galaria"– or in the modest country abode in Akrotiri, Marika Mitsotaki was in the process of learning not only how to cook fish –now one of her specialties– but also how to live up to her responsibilities as the spouse of a fast rising, dynamic young politician.

# From the "Galaria" in Crete to Glyfada in Athens

"My mother loved Marika very much," says Kostas Mitsotakis. "I had no father, he had passed away early on. All my family loved her but she too was very sociable and in good terms with everyone. Of course, she believed that they thought of her as an outsider, that as far as they were concerned, she would always be 'the Athenian', but the truth of the matter is that from the very first time that I took her to Crete, when we were still engaged and I was taking her to feasts and weddings, everywhere really, she responded wonderfully even if this was not the kind of life she was used to. Witness the fact that everybody always addressed her as Mrs. Marika, never Mrs. Mitsotaki. And that happens everywhere, not just in Crete, even today. My family, who has always been very important to me, loved her very much. One afternoon, as my mother lay dying in the hospital, she said to Marika:

"'My child, I am dying and I am leaving my family in your care. Make sure it stays united.'

"His sister Kaiti was his favorite," said Marika Mitsotaki in an interview to *Ta Nea* newspaper for a special feature on large Greek families. "He adored her, they grew up together. And I truly regret the fact that she never lived to see her brother become a prime minister. Kostas had three other siblings, Haralampos, Lefteris and Artemisia, spouse of G. Lymperakis."

The family is directly descendent from Eleftherios Venizelos, since Kostis Mitsotakis, Kostas' grandfather, married Katingo Venizelou, sister of Eleftherios.

"When we married, his family thought that I was a spoiled only child. Yet I came to live in a huge house that was so cold in the winter that I had to wear flannel nightdresses which I'd never worn before –in winter I would get cold sores…"

• The "Galaria", Kostas Mitsotakis' parents' home in Crete. It is older than the building that housed the family of Eleftherios Venizelos, the charismatic statesman and builder of modern Greece in the early 20th century.

Stories and memories from the Mitsotakis home in Crete abound. It came to be called "Galaria" because it had ballustraded balconies. Grandmother Stavroula resided permanently there, as were Kostas' older sister and her family, and also his younger brother, Lefteris, a doctor. "We, as well as Kostas' other siblings, would come during Easter and in the summer," says Marika Mitsotaki. "I remember, once, his brother Lefteris asked me to cook chicken with okra. I bought a fresh chicken and all the other necessary ingredients, cooked it, left it in the pot in the kitchen and went out. After a while, I see Lefteris and he says: 'It's the first time I've seen a one-legged chicken!' I was taken aback but he was right after all, because the chicken was actually missing a leg! You see, there were many people coming and going in the house and you could never be sure that things left unattended would remain intact! We all used to tease each other over this. For instance, Kaiti, Kostas' favorite sister, acquired the nickname 'Voutihtopoulou'* because she had such a soft spot for her youngest daughter, Ifigeneia, that whenever she would come across a delicacy, she would take it and hide it so she could give it to her later!"

Alexandra and Katerina, who are present in our conversation, have many memories from their childhood years in Crete: There was uncle Nondas, for example, aunt Kaiti's husband, who would always bring to the children a big box full of chocolate bars –this invariably made a great impression to the children and as a result his arrival was always an eagerly anticipated event... There was

* Roughly translates as "Lady Pilfering".

grandmother Stavroula and her famous home-made marmalades. She would also prepare a delicious tomato juice sprinkled with olive oil and salt, for the children to savor with warm bread fresh from the bakery, after their morning swim.

"The only custom that I was unable to take a liking to," continues Marika Mitsotaki, "was that for Easter they would have boiled lamb, not roasted on a spit, while after the Vigil for the Resurrection the main dish was tripe soup and lamb fricassee. In Crete they did not know how to spit roast. But I insisted and had two small pits dug in the courtyard of the 'Galaria', so we would be able to roast lamb and 'kokoretsi' in the traditional way!"

"Those were happy years, with the children coming one by one. Dora was first, followed by Alexandra two years later, then Katerina and finally, many years later, Kyriakos… by accident! Actually I wanted to have a large family

but the doctors had told me to be very careful because of the problems resulting from polio. My spine was very delicate; it could not support heavy loads…"

All the while Kostas Mitsotakis was carefully nurturing his career in politics, dividing his time between Parliament –never missing a day– and his electoral district, which he visited regularly. This meant he had to sail to Crete and back almost every week. All in all, there was hardly any time left for the family and the usual daily routines of married couples.

"We did not even have our own house though we wanted to," he explains. "When in Crete, we would either stay at the 'Galaria' or rent the little house in Akrotiri, while in Athens we had the house in Glyfada which was very small. In fact, it was the garage of Marika's parents' house which we got as part of her dowry. All that area belonged to her grandfather. Then an aunt of hers gave us another piece of land, so we built an extension to the existing structure and finally had a house that just barely managed to cover our needs. It was a 'piecemeal' house, as I used to call it. Another landplot was sold to

Onassis. It was in the Glyfada house that we held our wedding. Everybody came, even former Prime Minister Plastiras though he was very sick by then…"

"Talking about Onassis, I remember another priceless story, the one with the pig's head!" says Dora Bakoyanni, joining the conversation. "It is May 21, 1966 –my father's name day– and I'd been allowed to stay up late with the grownups. All our friends and relatives from Crete had come in early and they were eating and dancing and time was passing by pleasantly when suddenly, at one thirty a.m., the doorbell rang. It was Onassis who was living nearby in Glyfada. After wishing my father all the best, he turned and asked my mother:

"'Is there anything to eat, Marikaki? I'm hungry!'

"My mother proceeded to scold him like she would a misbehaving child: 'You should be ashamed of yourself,' she said to him. 'You have the best of everything and yet there is nothing in your house for you to eat?'

"In the end, after she finished giving him a piece of her mind, she said:

"'There's a pig's head –you can have that if you want to.'

"And so, Onassis sat and ate the pig's head."

Gradually the tradition to entertain at the garden of the house in Glyfada took root: initially with the wedding of the Mitsotakises, then with name days and all other occasions for joyous celebration –weddings, christenings, anniversaries, children's parties and, nowadays, great grandchildren's parties. After all, the one undisputed rule during all these years, a rule followed always and everywhere, has been for the family to make the effort to come together around the table and feel as one.

• Wearing life jackets during evacuation practice onboard. Marika is the only one not wearing hers.
• A lovely snapshot of the children during their summer vacations in Crete. Unfortunately, those carefree days would come to an end a short while later...

# Hard times

Greece would wake up to a cacophony of unfamiliar sounds on the 21st of April 1967: the rattle of armored vehicle tractor treads on the asphalt, martial music, paranoid announcements from the Armed Forces –they all composed a shocking prelude to the ills that were to follow…

Word-of-mouth quickly spread the unexpected piece of news among civilians: "There's been a coup". The night before there had been arrests of civilians and all soldiers' leaves were revoked.

"Long after we had gone to bed we heard noise outside our bedroom: it was the stomp of footsteps…" remembers Marika Mitsotaki. "I was the first to dart out of bed and rushed to open the bedroom door. In a split second I realized that there were soldiers standing on the other side, their guns aimed at me. I shut the door back again, locking it as well! Then Kostas said:

"'It's pointless, really, just open the door…'

"So we opened the door and he asked the soldiers:

"'What is it you lads want?'

"Because indeed they were all very young, barely out of adolescence.

"'We've come to arrest you,' they shouted, 'quick, come as you are, in your pajamas'.

"'That's outrageous,' Kostas protested, 'even the Germans allowed me to dress when they arrested me during the Occupation.'

"But the soldiers had their orders, they were jerking him around violently, pushing us this way and that, really rough behavior… The children woke up and watched what was happening, frightened… Kostas only managed to change into a pair of pants, he was taken away wearing his pajama top. It was 2 a.m. when they left and the first thing I noticed was that they had broken in by bashing the locks of the main entrance door as well as the bedroom's, using the butt end of their rifles. I was left alone with three children, speechless, horrified.

"Devastated, I sat in our living room as people from neighboring apartments started coming in. I shall never forget Mrs. Zaimis who kept on repeating, 'It's terrible, it's terrible…' She went on and on in a monotone, for so long that in the end it started sounding ridiculous. Our friend, Takis Eliadis, also came in and after sitting with us for a while, visibly shaken, went to the fridge, opened it, took out a dish with zucchini, brought it in the sitting room and absentmindedly started eating one zucchini after another! Anyway, the phones were not working, the lines had already been cut off and we had no way of communicating with the outside world to find out exactly what was happening. My father, however, somehow found out about Kostas' arrest –or perhaps he just suspected it would happen– and he came as soon as he could. A little before daybreak, I lay down to try to calm my nerves a little bit but, really, I was petrified with fear. They had taken away Kostas and I had no idea what they were going to do to him. Moreover, I had no idea of what *we* were going to do.

"Plucking up all my courage, I started trying to locate Kostas the very next day. The only thing I knew was that he was held in Pikermi, a suburb some 20 km outside Athens. I met a lot of people in key positions, I even went all the way to Ioannis Ladas, who was the commanding officer of ESA, the Greek Military Police, and a henchman of the *junta*. Three days later, I was finally given the much desired permit to visit my husband at a specific time. Thankfully, he was in good health and with typical Mitsotakian humor gave me a detailed account of his arrest. He stayed at Pikermi for a short length of time and then he was brought back home, where he remained under confinement for six months.

"This was not easy for any of us at first. It was especially difficult for the children to accept the new situation with their father a prisoner in his own house, unable to go out or receive any guests. But they grew used to it bit by bit. Fortunately, their friends and fellow pupils were free to visit.

"It was a difficult period, hours and days unfolding at a crawling pace. We read books to pass the time and discussed the same things over and over, because there was no inflow of news. In the evenings neighbors living in the same building would often come to keep us company.

"The truth is that we had help from everyone –from the Zaimis family, from actress Anna Synodinou and her husband, from Giorgos Marinakis– and we kept our patience as we waited for developments. One of the things we regularly discussed was how would Kostas find a way to go to Paris, where politicians and intellectuals were slowly converging, self-exiles in central Europe, trying to organize a resistance movement against the generals from outside Greece's borders. The plan was to sail to Turkey with a small-sized boat and then fly out from there. I insisted that he should wait until the holiday of the 15th of August, when the increased traffic of boats big and small would boost his chances to slip through undetected. It was a dangerous plan…"

"I was certain that there would be a dictatorship, before it happened in April of 1967," adds Kostas Mitsotakis, "and I knew that they were going to arrest me but I was not taking any precautions, I kept sleeping normally at home. I remember that two days before my arrest, Marika woke me up in the middle of the night, sat cross-legged on the bed and said:

"'I can't decide whether you are careless or foolish! Since you know that they are going to arrest you, why are you still staying here?'

"What happened next is a matter of record. I was arrested willy-nilly and transported to the Armored Vehicles Central Command in Pikermi, then was imprisoned in my own house, and then, well, I never slept in my bed again! I had put in place a network of friends who would hide me, unbeknownst to each other, until I managed to escape to Paris."

"Among the things that I found very upsetting, during the time that Kostas was under house arrest," says Marika Mitsotaki, "were the attempts of our 'keepers' to humiliate us –me especially. I was permitted to go out but alone, of course, without my husband, and I felt helpless against their affronts. One day, as I was returning home from the market at noontime, the policeman guarding us started hurling insults at me. It was the practice then for the guards to

• The girls and their father in an excursion to Mystras, in the spring of 1968, shortly before he left for Paris. They were photographed by Giorgos Marinakis, a neighbor and dear friend.

act as *agents provocateurs*, trying to incite some sort of reaction from you that would give them the right to punish you afterwards."

"I must admit that on that day I got very angry and said to him:

"'You'd better watch your language because I'll have you leave this place feet-first!'

"Well, did I ever regret saying that… Two days later, I received a summons to Military Court. Courts martial were nothing to laugh about those days… Naturally, the children were terrified at the thought that they would be losing

their mother as well –everyone was panicking at home. The court sentenced me to four months in jail, so my defense attorney, in order to make matters a bit easier for me, threw his own surprise bomb in court saying:

"'However, I would like to ask the honorable justices to take into consideration the fact that Mrs. Marika is pregnant.'

"Everyone in the courtroom froze – in the end I got a suspended sentence."

Indeed, the Mitsotakises were getting ready to welcome into the family a new member, namely Kyriakos. On March 1968, eleven months after the coup put Greece under a seven-year dictatorship, Marika Mitsotaki gave birth to the son that she so wanted to present to her husband, overlooking the fact that her spine was too fragile to go through another pregnancy and against Kostas Mitsotakis' objections that it could further damage her health.

"When I got pregnant with Kyriakos, I went to my doctor, Antonis Komninos and said to him:

"'Open the window so I can jump off!'

"'Whatever for?' he asked me.

"'Because I think I am pregnant and under the circumstances I do not think I can keep this child.'

"It was a very difficult time for us. There was the *junta*, Mitsotakis was under house arrest and I was not in the best of health.

"'You are indeed pregnant,' he confirmed, 'but you shall bring your pregnancy to term and you shall have a beautiful boy!'

"And the funny thing is that, while the deliveries of the girls had given me a hard time, Kyriakos came into the world in half an hour. I remember that, after he came out, I checked again and again to make sure that he was a boy. Those days, my mother was living near the Elena Maternity Hospital. After taking me there at around 4 in the morning so I would be readied for labor, Kostas went over to my mother's for a quick cup of coffee. He had barely arrived at her house when he received word that the baby had been delivered! I'll never forget how he came running as I was shouting out from afar:

"'Kosta, I bore you a son!'

"He had no problem with the girls, but I did want to give him a son."

"She had been advised not to have any children and yet she had four! I think what saved her was the fact that she did put on very little weight during her pregnancies," says Kostas Mitsotakis. "Actually, later in Paris she wanted us to have a fifth child so that Kyriakos would have company but I said to her, 'I think you're out of your mind!' However, she was totally against the matter of abortion and that is why, when she got pregnant with Kyriakos, she would have kept the child no matter what. After the altercation with the policeman and the military trial, I asked her doctor to prepare a statement about her pregnancy so that she would be spared imprisonment. We could not afford to have Marika be away from the family. She was always a wonderfully supporting partner for me and an exceptional mother to our children. She devoted her whole life to us."

# Sailing to salvation

In the summer of 1968, after giving birth to Kyriakos, Marika Mitsotaki proved once more that she was willing to assist her husband, even if that meant paying a heavy price for it. To divert attention from Kostas Mitsotakis and facilitate his escape to Paris, she travelled to Crete with Dora, Katerina and the baby, and had Alexandra go to the island of Zakynthos, accompanied by her husband's secretary, Eleni Galati. The officers at the Central Intelligence Service (CIS) were on tenterhooks as they tried to determine his whereabouts.

"On the eve of the holiday of August 15th," she remembers, "police officers came to the 'Galaria', our house in Crete and told me, 'Take the children and come with us, we've been ordered to send you back to Athens.'

"They were ready to bundle us up and take us to the airport right there and then. I stood my ground saying 'I'm not going anywhere'. My brother-in-law, a doctor, was staying at the other end of the house. Hearing the commotion, he came running and asked for explanations:

"'She is a woman alone with three kids –what is it you want from her?'

"One of the men in uniform was a bit more conciliatory, as Kostas and I had been best man and woman at his wedding. 'Kyria Marika,' he said, 'please, say nothing and don't make any fuss –our orders are to take you to Athens,' and all the while he was murmuring to himself, 'My, oh my, oh my, what shall I say to my wife this evening?'

"The police officers boarded the plane with us so I said to them mockingly: 'Good idea not to leave me alone because I might take a parachute and jump off the plane with my kids in tow!' When we landed in Athens Hellinikon Airport, I spotted my father from afar. He was waiting for us anxiously, because he had heard the news but he was not allowed to approach us. My mother was standing beside him. Though as a person she was generally controlled and unemotional, she suddenly started screaming hysterically, 'oh my child, my child!' right there in the middle of the arrivals area and then, amid all the shouting, she throws herself in my arms, hugs me and whispers in my ear: 'Kostas has left'. She had staged this frenzied act just to pass on to me the information that my husband had managed to escape. I wasn't sure whether I should be happy or sad with the news…

"When the police officers asked us where we wanted them to take us I said, 'Take us to Glyfada, our home'. Upon arriving there, they asked everyone to go away saying, 'No one is allowed to stay, everyone must go, including the German woman.' By that they meant our dear Nane, the nanny who was taking care of Kyriakos, as she had done with all the other children ever since they were born, as I could not lift them up, among other things, owing to my health problems. It took some effort to make the policemen understand why the nanny should not go and leave the baby by itself… 'Well, then,' they said, 'she should sign a statement that she is staying of her own accord,' which of course she did immediately.

"The telephone line had been disconnected and so once more we found ourselves cut off from the outside world. Early next morning, a little after we got up from bed, we saw Kostas' brother, Haralampos, waiting for us outside the garden fence. He waited for me to go a little closer to the fence and then he called out, within earshot of all the policemen around us:

"'Hello there, Marika, how's everyone? Do you need me to get you anything from the market?'

"In other words he started chit chatting with me until at a certain moment he silently mouthed the words: 'Kostas has arrived'. You see, as soon as Mitsotakis reached the coast of Turkey, at Cesme, he sent a one-word telegram to his brother, a secret code word they had agreed upon, just so we knew he had made it. Meanwhile, the children, the nanny and I remained confined in Glyfada without any contact with the outside world. Until one morning we woke up to find that, miraculously, the policemen had disappeared. Much to the amazement of the children, one of them had actually left his rifle behind!"

In a sense, Kostas Mitsotakis was also free but in exile and with zero possibilities of returning home, for the moment at least. To make his painful getaway to freedom, he had to cross the sea channel between the island of Chios and the Turkish coastline at night on the eve of the holiday of the 15th of August, aboard a small vessel called Sotiria*.

"The 'Sotiria' was a 10-meter, Chris-Craft-type boat, with two diesel-powered engines,' he remembers. "A friend of Andreas Papandreou had bought it to facilitate his escape but things turned out differently, as usually happens in life. In the end, Papandreou left Greece officially carrying a passport, while the 'Sotiria' was bought by one of my friends so I could escape from the *junta*, on that night of August 15th in 1968… The night before, the meltemi winds were so strong that, had they held, our crossing would not have been possible. Travelling with me was a friend, an Italian-Yugoslav, who was supposed to be the skipper but I, clueless though I was in sea matters, knew more about navigation than he did!"

They sailed off from Rafina in the middle of the night and headed for the Kafirea Narrows, the infamous Cavo d'Oro passage, with the seas still rough and rolling. Those few that were in on the scheme, thought the idea was simply crazy. "Have you any idea how many miles it is to Turkey?" they'd ask. "You'll

* "Salvation" in Greek.

run out of fuel." So the two passengers of the "Sotiria" loaded the boat with fuel drums, which actually further increased the risks.

They braved the rough waters all night until around daybreak, as they were closing in on Chios, they caught sight of the regular transport boat that connected the island with Piraeus. On Mitsotakis' suggestion they maneuvered their craft behind the ship to take advantage of the calmer waters in its trail, but after a while they changed course and headed for Cesme on the Turkish coast, where the local authorities helped the self-exiled politician leave for Paris.

"Temporarily at least the worst was behind us," says Marika Mitsotaki. "But we faced terrible difficulties because of the *junta*... Additionally, we had financial problems and I had to sell off an apartment on Ioannou Drosopoulou Street. I handled all these matters myself, because communicating with Kostas was a very complicated affair. We had arranged to have at our disposal 5 or 6 secret telephone lines interspersed throughout Athens –at an office branch of the National Bank of Greece, for example. I would go in, call Kostas, then I would sneak out from the back door like a burglar. I knew I was constantly under surveillance and I remember that, several years later, we would be walking down the street with the children and they would automatically turn their head every now and then to check if anyone was following us. They were afraid.

"There were many problems and as usually happens when things turn sour, most of our acquaintances disappeared. I lived in the house alone with the children and I would go out on very few occasions, together with relatives or some of the few friends that kept contact with us. We usually went for a stroll and then ended up having lunch or dinner at a small taverna.

"I went through a lot, but if I were to live my life again I would still want to be with Kostas, even if that meant going through tough times again. To me, there is no one else like him in the whole world. Funnily enough, although he is supposed to be proverbially cool-headed, I –deeply sentimental and volatile by nature– remained unperturbed throughout that era, eyeing things with a philosopher's reserve... Perhaps what helped me was the fact that I never had negative thoughts, never allowed myself to imagine the worst possible scenario..."

# Reunited

Meanwhile, Paris had become a shining beacon of the Greek resistance to the *junta* of the generals. Many luminaries from the fields of politics, culture and the arts had formed a *sui generis* community that, among others, worked to spread the message around the world that democracy and freedom had to return to the land that begat them. Back in Athens, though, the mood was one of darkness and desperation; those were the barren years of the dictatorship.

"The children were asking for their father," Marika Mitsotaki points out, "and it was normal after all, they missed him. There was also the fact that they had come to see him as a hero, after what he had been through. As for myself, I was feverishly trying to figure out a way to re-unite the family. It was a challenging task, however, because the *junta* would not issue us passports.

"Both Kostas in Paris and I in Athens were making efforts to get these much needed travel documents. Speaking about our confinement in one of his press interviews, Kostas aptly pointed out that 'our son, who is 6 months old, is probably the world's youngest political prisoner'.

"And yet it seemed that the *junta* would never issue us the passports we needed so much. So we put in place a plan to escape using counterfeit documents in the coming summer, when suddenly I received a call from the office of Pattakos, one of the principals of the *junta*. He wanted to see me, they said. I went there immediately and upon seeing me enter he announced pompously:

"'Thanks to the magnanimity of our president, Georgios Papadopoulos, you may obtain a passport and leave the country.'

"To which I replied with covert irony:

"'Please convey my warmest thanks to the president.'

"Ecstatic, I rushed back home and I started packing with such speed and excitement that honestly, to this day, I cannot remember how I did it… Luckily we found tickets for a ship that was passing through Piraeus the following day, on its way to Venice. I remember that the ship had barely cast anchor when I barged in with our old Mercedes and all the gang –the four children and the German nanny. What a treasure that woman was… She would not even consider getting paid all the time that we were exiled in Paris.

"So we went aboard, got settled in our cabin and then set off on what I came to call my 'voyage of yearning'. We loved each other very much, Kostas and I, and it was very hard for us to stay apart for so long, for a year minus one month actually.

"As the ship sailed into Venice and was closing in on the Rialto –that's where boats used to berth in those days– we all rushed to the deck's railing and leaned over it, trying to spot Kostas on the pier below. And there he was, waiting for us!… Everyone was crying. The children and Nane were the first to disembark and I followed with the car fully loaded with our luggage. Then the seven of us squeezed inside it –it was like a scene from an Italian movie– with Kostas at the wheel, me and one child sitting beside him and Nane with the three children in the back seat.

"Summer was almost over and I remember that suddenly there was a storm. We were driving north but it started raining so hard that we had to stop and take shelter under a bridge for a considerable length of time, because visibility was almost zero.

"When the rain subsided, we resumed our drive to Paris by way of Milan, jammed-packed inside the car like so many sardines."

• Marika and the children enjoying a short respite on their way to Paris to re-unite with their father. Baby Kyriakos, on Dora's lap, has not been baptized yet.

# In Paris

In Paris Kostas Mitsotakis had rented a small, typically Parisian apartment, which was also sunny and very clean. It was located in a very good arrondissement, the 16th –1 Rue Mirabeau, 3rd floor– and it was overlooking the Place de Barcelone, a small, tree-lined square, with an old, typical French café in the middle.

"Every morning we would wake up to the song of nightingales," remembers Marika Mitsotaki, wistfully. "From the very first day I decided to make our life there as good as possible. First, we tried to find a school for the children, a German one preferably, like the one they were attending in Athens. Things were difficult at first but in the end we got to adapt –the children especially. As for myself, I've always believed in the old adage that home is wherever you lay your head to sleep. The way I interpret it is that home is where the family is and that, wherever that may be, you should try to make the best of it. In Paris, the children used to go to walks with their father and, most importantly, they would have long conversations with him. It was as if they were getting to know their father all over again. I remember these days with nostalgia…

"There were many other exiled Greeks like us in Paris. Of course, we all believed that at a certain point things would change and that we would all be able to return to Greece.

"When summer came the first time around, we thought it would not be prudent to send the children to spend their vacations in Crete, fearing that they would not be allowed to return to us. So we all went together to a very pretty village in what was then communist Yugoslavia. We stayed there for almost a whole month, but there was nothing to eat, the food was terrible and we literally went hungry. Alexandra, who was thin to begin with, got to be just skin and bones. Once, the children noticed that the restaurant catalog listed spaghetti with Napolitana sauce and they were delighted because they thought they would finally get to

• Marika, her mother, Katerina and Kyriakos in Paris.

eat some real food. But when the spaghetti arrived, a small portion in a small side dish and cold at that, their hearts sank. Kostas, who was tired of hearing us complain about being hungry, went to the local supermarket and managed to find eggs and the ingredients for a Greek country salad. And actually he made for us some huge salads himself! One time he had to go to Rome for some business and brought back some small cheese rounds and chocolate bars, which he would give out to the children one at a time, like we did during the Occupation. After that experience, we sent the children to Crete for the summer holidays.

"While in Paris, I honed my cooking skills. When you like something, you make it a point to stay informed and I was a careful observer of French cuisine in restaurants, in private homes, everywhere. We would, often, invite friends over and we'd cook; this gave us much joy. One night I pan fried forty pieces of salt cod! I ended up smelling like a cod myself! Salt cod accompanied with 'skordalia' garlic sauce is Kostas' favorite food. I remember that on that night, among the many friends who had come over, were composer Mikis Theodorakis, author Alki Zei and the late scholar Marios Ploritis. We had so much fun in those get-togethers… Among the pleasant memories that Paris gave us were the Sunday lunches when we used to cook our favorite dishes: chicken with rice, *schnitzel*, roast beef, or some nice fresh fish that Kostas had got from the street market where he went invariably."

"France was a very interesting experience, in many ways," Kostas Mitsotakis concurs. "It is there, for example, that I learned how to pick good wine and how to shop for meat. It's a special skill, something that must be learned. We do not know how to cut meat properly here. I learned, for instance, that good, tender parts for boiled meat are the trotters and the ribs but the absolute best is the tail!

"In Paris we had an old car that was very much like an armored vehicle! It was a second-hand Rover that we bought after our Mercedes sort of… kicked the bucket after the trip from Greece! So we used the Rover to go to the street market every Saturday to get supplies and that's where I found out to my great surprise that the French do not eat suckling pig.

"We usually bought our meat from the same vendor and one day, upon seeing us buying suckling pig for the nth time, the seller asked Marika:

"'So you eat this? How do you prepare it?'

"Marika gave her the recipe, together with some tips and when the seller tried the recipe at home, her family just loved it!

"I had discovered a co-op food shop where I usually gave the assistant a five-franc tip and he would bend over backwards trying to help us carry the bags to the car or whatever… You see, the French are rather tight-fisted, they do not tip much. Once, looking at the quantities we bought, he asked me:

"'You're a restaurant owner, right?'

"So I answered: 'No, I just have a large family!'"

• Kyriakos' christening took place in the "City of Light" –and of self-exile. Kyriakos is held by his paternal grandmother, Stavroula.

"Many years later, when my grand-daughter Alexia was studying in Paris and I happened to be in the city, I was doing the shopping for meat. I used to buy really good cuts for the famous French *pot-au-feu*. Often I would also buy fish. It is there that I got to know about turbot which in Greece we call 'kalkani' –a species that the French would not eat in earlier times because it is truly ugly-looking! Marica absolutely loves all shell-fish, while I love clams. Generally, I prefer classic French cuisine, not the rather pretentious 'nouvelle cuisine'.

"Marika is right when she says that in Paris I got to really know my children. They went to an excellent German language school in the suburb of Saint Cloud. It is with me that they learned what it means to engage in dialogue, something that we Greeks do not know how to do well. We lived frugally in a small house, but you can make a life in Paris no matter what your finances are. In my first year there I lived alone. Thankfully, I had a Portuguese housekeeper who knew how to cook salt cod in fifty different ways!

"France expanded our culinary vocabulary. We learned many things that we did not know of here in Greece. Marika used to cook regularly and we had many loyal customers, as it were! One of them was Constantinos Karamanlis who came very often for dinner. It is amazing how he managed to keep his body weight constant. I used to put on weight as the years went by, but he didn't. When he lived in Paris, he would have new suits sewn for him in Athens without having to go through fittings. His measurements were always the same. The truth is he was a very moderate eater. He especially liked Macedonian pie, leafy-greens pie, feta cheese and all the Greek pot roasts and stews that his man-servant Theodoros used to prepare. His favorite sweet was the *babas au rhum* that Marika used to make for him. He drank only red wine and, much to the chagrin of the French sommeliers, he drank it with fish as well –with added ice cubs no less! A sacrilege!

"In the end, Paris gave us bittersweet memories. It stands alone as a period, being completely different from all other times of our lives. The children especially benefited from it. But exile is hard, like an open-ended prison sentence.

You do not know if you'll ever return home. And yet we did enjoy our time in Paris. On the whole, we have good memories from every place we've been. This is one of the many things we share, Marika and I.

"Generally, I never get anxious, as I also never feel fear. This is how I've dealt with all adversities in my life. Come Saturday night, I would roll down the blinds, as it were, to keep worries out and I would declare 'I shall deal with any outstanding matters on Monday'. I never took worries back home with me. I was this way since I was a little boy.

"Marika and I had many common interests to begin with and acquired even more in the course of our relationship. But we do not agree on everything. For instance, she adores ballet and music

• Food-wise the family's vacation in Yugoslavia was a complete disaster.

–after all she studied ballet before contracting polio– which I am not very fond of, while on the other hand I adore the theatre which she does not care much about. But we do love cinema, reading, travelling, collecting old objects and of course, good food. Marika was always interested in politics; she would get very passionate about it and also had good instinct. She is an extremely astute judge of character. I may have been wrong sometimes –not she."

On September 1973, four years after the famous "voyage of yearning", the Mitsotakises prepared to return home, taking advantage of the fact that martial law had been repealed by the Markezinis administration.

"I was the first to leave," Marika remembers, "along with the children and Nane and, the truth is, I was crying throughout the flight home. I was worried that we would get tangled up in politics again. Though our life in exile was certainly not problem-free, I knew for certain that our carefree days were over…"

Marika Mitsotaki's premonition was right. After the return to Greece –a move that the family had been fervently looking forward to– serious political developments occured: the student uprising at the Athens Polytechnic in November 1973, brought the armed forces back in Athens and a new, much more brutal *junta* was established. Kostas Mitsotakis was persecuted once more and he wound up in prison again, this time in Chania, Crete. He was freed in the summer of 1974, when the *junta* fell and normal political life resumed. What followed next, came as an unpleasant surprise for many: Notwithstanding the fact that, throughout his exile in Paris, Mitsotakis had been a fervent advocate of the plan to have Karamanlis return to Greece to organize the restoration of democratic political practices, in the end he found himself not only out of the new Karamanlis administration, but out of parliament as well.

# The house in Crete

However, as so often happens in life, and as Kostas Mitsotakis also believes, "Every cloud has a silver lining". And the truth of the matter is that those few years away from parliament allowed the couple to turn their attention to the family estate. After liquidating certain real estate holdings, they managed to acquire their own home in Akrotiri, in the city of Chania, only a few kilometers away from Mitsotakis' paternal home, the "Galaria".

"We hired a good architect, university professor Dimitri Antonakakis," he says. "He supplied the design esthetic and we worked in the functional requirements. The building has domes, which constitute one of the main characteristics of Cretan architecture. When construction was completed, Marika went to Crete with three other women and within a week she managed to have it fully equipped and furnished down to the last detail, including the flower arrangements!"

Marika Mitsotaki is equally proud of the house in Akrotiri and of her garden in particular.

"Where once there was, really, noth-

• Crete: Holiday cakes and biscuits are arranged atop the old cupboard. On the wall above, hangs a beautiful hand-embroidered cloth from Marika's collection.

ing but rocks, we created an amazing garden. There was nary a tree in there and now you have the impression that you are entering Athens' Botanical Garden. I put in a lot of my heart and soul in this garden and it gives me great pleasure to take it all in from my veranda, as I know each and every single tree in it, each and every single plant. We have figs, oranges, lemons, apricots, pears –though regrettably we do not get to savor much of the latter, as the birds get to them first. This house is a source of great joy for us. After all, nothing is more important than family…"

She uses the word "family" in its full, true sense. Because, in fact, the story of the "Galaria" and what it came to be –a welcoming haven and meeting point for three generations that co-existed under one roof, children and cousins coming together during Easter and summer holidays, sheer pandemonium being the order of the day at times– is repeated today in the house in Akrotiri.

She goes on:

"We built our house at the right time. Our daughters had gotten married and had had their kids. All our grandchildren grew up here. As a young child, Kyriakos –the last of the brood and feeling perhaps more of an only child– would invite over his numerous playmates. Today it is our great-grandchildren who come and once again, space seems to be in short supply! But we did manage to find space for our splendid collections, a labor of love, with pieces from all over Greece and all parts of the world."

"Collecting old artifacts," adds Kos-

• The old wooden chest and the decorative objects on it are part of the Marika Mitsotaki collection.

tas Mitsotakis, "was a favorite pursuit of both of us since the early years of our marriage. We collected maps of Crete, religious icons, textiles, copper ware, all kinds of folk art and, of course, our Minoan Collection which we donated to the Chania Museum many years ago."

"When we are in Crete," says Marika Mitsotaki, "there are two things that Kostas will invariably do and we all find this habit very amusing. Though he hardly knows how to boil an egg, as it were, and though he has no aptitude for fixing things around the house, he does have two specialties: preparing vinaigrette salad dressing and a Bloody Mary cocktail. The latter especially has evolved into a ritual that is repeated only on Sundays at noon and only in Crete –never in Athens and never at night! And according to the ritual's time-honored protocol, first we drink the cocktail and then we have a barbecue –no exceptions! This practice has become such a staple of our sojourns in Crete that everyone, our children, their friends and guests generally, arrange their schedules around it so they can be present at the... ceremony! Arrivals, departures and everything in-between are arranged in relation to the Bloody Mary cocktail and the barbecue. The preparation process itself is a sight to behold: all the ingredients –tomatoes, vodka, salt, pepper, Tabasco sauce– are laid out on the work surface and a serious-looking Mitsotakis mixes and blends them with the air of a grand priest! Anticipation for the event starts from around ten in the morning when the older grandchildren start nagging him:

"'You haven't forgotten that today is a Sunday, have you, Grandpa?' they ask.

"And when the famous cocktail is ready, it is expected that everyone shall drink –no exceptions!"

"Not only is drinking it obligatory," adds Kyriakos Mitsotakis laughing, "but comments and suggestions are not allowed either. I got a disapproving look once when I asked him to use less vodka, as alcohol can be a bit too much for the stomach on hot summer days. In fact, not only does he refuse to use a smaller quantity of vodka than the one mentioned in the recipe, but adds some more for good measure!"

"They can make fun of me all they want," adds Kostas Mitsotakis laughing, "but they do beg me to prepare it every single time. Aside from this, there are other practices that the house in Crete has allowed us to make a habit of. When I was a child for instance, meals were taken with the whole family sitting at the table, at specific times too. This is what we try to keep doing as much as possible today. There is a practical reason for this as well, because when you prepare food for twenty, you just can't have everyone coming in for dinner whenever they please. When in Athens, the family disperses; we rarely manage to round up a big group. But here we do try to bring in everyone. My grandchildren alone –bless 'em– are thirteen! Thankfully we found a big,

long table, like the ones in monasteries, that sits fourteen."

"Indeed," agrees Alexandra, "one needs to negotiate long and hard to get lunch to be served if only half an hour later, at 2:30 say, instead of 2:00. The strongest argument of Grandma and Grandpa is that they cook their grand children's favorite foods. I recently heard my sons say: 'Sure, we want to go have a swim at Falasairna but not at the cost of missing filet with mushroom sauce!' "

"What is very interesting, even today," concludes Kostas Mitsotakis, "are the stimulating conversations we have when we are all at the table. And when it comes to debating, Marika is usually the least democratic, as it were. I remember once she was disagreeing with Dora –who was sixteen at the time and already taking the opposing view on everything– on an encyclopedic matter about which my daughter was actually right. To prove her point, Dora got up and brought a volume of the *Encyclopedia Britannica* and showed to her mother the entry in question. And yet even that was not good enough for Marika: "Well then, you should get another encyclopedia", she shot back, leaving the rest of us speechless! Our discussions were always rather heated but I never forced my children to agree with me. They had their own views and we often disagreed, but I would listen carefully to what they had to say because they all have good, strong minds."

Therefore, amid the discussions and the disagreements and the ground rules, there is one single house rule

–fundamental and authentically Greek– that keeps families together, even when the going gets rough: the blessed meeting around the table where the food, be it abundant or meager, becomes link and balm, a source of support and hope. That is the reason why in political or familial difficult times, from the early days of the "Galaria" to Glyfada to the exile in Paris up until today and the house in Crete, one inviolable rule of the Mitsotakis household has been for all the members to gather around the table as often as possible –a rule that undoubtedly contributed to the family keeping its unity.

"I feel so proud when I see us all together here in Crete!" says Marika Mitsotaki, smiling broadly. "Four children, thirteen grandchildren and the great-grandchildren as well, they all congregate here in the Easter holidays or summer vacations and the house turns into a regular madhouse! One should also add friends and I don't mean just the locals –anyone who comes to Crete makes it a point to drop in. We'd be in the kitchen all day and the scents and aromas of our cooking will waft out and travel for miles around. In Easter the smell of barbecued meat drives everyone crazy with anticipation. We prepare lamb meat, goat meat, 'kokoretsi', caul-wrapped liver and sweetmeat rolls, spare ribs, mushroom pies, zucchini pies...Of course, a period of fasting is preceding all this so when the children start complaining I tell them: 'That's all there is for now and you should accept it!' In the end they manage to go through the fast eating French fries and 'taramosalata'*. Thankfully, all the children get along with each other very well, starting with Alexia –Dora's daughter and the eldest grandchild– and a mother herself already, down to Daphne –daughter of Kyriakos, who is the youngest. They are all very different from one another, but do not ask me who I love the most. Even if I supposedly do have favorites, these change from year to year and I love and feel deeply proud of all of them."

* Fish roe spread

• Kostas and Marika Mitsotaki share a passion for collecting traditional utensils.

# Snapshots and memories

So many happenings, so many joys and tribulations, so many memories…

How is it possible to trace a life's journey when it is so closely related to the country's most important events in recent post-war history? One can only furnish random snapshots of this journey, some relatively known, some not, many revolving around the family table, others having the kitchen as their starting point. Here we go then with snapshots and memories…

## Florakis and the non-existent "dolmadakia"

In 1989, as attempts were being made to form an all-party ecumenical government, the then leaders of the Left –Leonidas Kyrkos and Harilaos Florakis– met with Kostas Mitsotakis* at the latter's house in Glyfada. That meeting was to enter the annals under the heading "Marika's 'dolmadakia'": This traditional stuffed vine leaves dish briefly enjoyed first-page status thanks to the reported preference of Florakis for it, though "im-

* Kostas Mitsotakis was Prime Minister of Greece in the years 1990-1993.

• A snapshot from Dora's engagement, in the autumn of 1974. The Mitsotakises, center, are flanked by Marika's father, standing beside her, and Pavlos Bakoyannis.

agined preference" would be more accurate. As Marika Mitsotaki recalls, "there wasn't any dinner, it was an ordinary meeting and we served coffee and a sweet, nothing more. Naturally, there were reporters stationed outside and the following day I saw these first-page headlines about my 'dolmadakia'! It was a journalistic concoction, of course!"

A few years later, Florakis asked Mitsotakis: "Well, how about it? Won't you invite us over to get a taste of your wife's legendary 'dolmadakia'?"

"Unfortunately, we never had the chance," adds Kostas Mitsotakis.

### Regarding olive oil and Bush's "clandestine" cookies

In the summer of 1991, then President of the USA, George Bush and his wife Barbara, visited Crete for a day.

"Americans, even those in high positions, are typically very unassuming", says Marika Mitsotaki. "So when the Bushes visited the island, we had them over for lunch at our veranda dismissing protocol. Funnily and purely by coincidence, both Bush and Mitsotakis wore light-blue shirts and light-colored trousers, which made them look like very mature university students! For lunch we had lobster, pies and stuffed zucchini. They loved everything and what really impressed me was that afterwards they asked to meet the young women that had helped with the cooking and went over to the kitchen to congratulate them.

"Needless to say, two weeks earlier the security officials of the American

• Mitsotakis, honorary President of the New Democracy party, flanked by his mother –in the black and white dress– and Marika's mother.

president, had gone through our house with a fine-toothed comb, inspecting even the power outlets!

"On the eve of their arrival we were in the kitchen making preparations when the Bushes' bodyguards came in and started looking into the cooking pots, tasting everything to make sure that the president would not be poisoned. Additionally a special bodyguard was posted to keep watch over the refrigerators at night!"

"We actually came close to having a diplomatic incident when Bush's cook, a monstrously big fellow, attempted to come into the kitchen, which is my mother's exclusive domain!' adds Dora Bakoyanni. "She would have none of this 'foreign intervention' and in the end I had to step in as negotiator which proved to be a rather trying experience!"

And yet in the end, the perfectly trained and otherwise very efficient guardian angels of the President of the USA were undermined by Greek ingenuity, so to speak! Marika Mitsotaki smiles softly at the memory.

"Two days before the Bushes' visit, I was still in Athens. I was getting ready to leave at daybreak to catch the 7 a.m. flight to Chania when my mother handed me a box of her superb savory biscuits, one of her specialties. Two days later, as we sat with the Bushes at our veranda sipping traditional ouzo, I served these, well, effectively clandestine biscuits which had not gone through any security check. And actually the American president liked them so much that he immediately christened them 'mommy's cookies' and ate almost all of them!"

But this was not the only funny episode from the Bushes' visit to Crete. Here is another one in Dora Bakoyanni's words:

"We had taken our seats around the table and the salads were served first. Bush takes a mouthful and goes crazy over the olive oil dressing! So what is the classic response of Greeks –and Cretans no less– when someone praises their local products? They offer them to you as a gift –in this case two 20-kilo tin cans! These, however, could not be taken by the Bushes aboard the legendary Air Force One aircraft because –for security reasons, of course– absolutely nothing edible is allowed into the aircraft from any of the places it lands. "No problem," we said and proceeded to arrange for the olive oil to reach the White House by way of our embassy in the

• Standing beside Kostas Mitsotakis is Emma, the proud assistant cook and co-mistress of the realm of the kitchen, who has just been congratulated by US President Bush. On the far right is Mrs. Eleni and Mr. Nikos, the cook.

USA, and thought no more of it. Six months later my parents and I went to Paris to attend a very important official function. I remember that then French President Mitterand had arranged for the event to take place at the Versailles Palace and they pulled out all the stops to create a very impressive atmosphere of splendor. We were in the Hall of Mirrors listening to Gorbachev's address when I was approached by a Marine, sporting the usual crew-cut, who said to me politely but sternly: 'President Bush would like to have a word with you.'

"As soon as I had the chance, I left my seat and went up to the American president who upon seeing me said:

"'The oil that you were to send to us has not reached us yet'.

"Furious at the news, we summoned Manousos –Kostas Mitsotakis' loyal and devoted bodyguard, effectively his guardian angel for decades– and gave him a piece of our minds! The man kept insisting –and rightly so– that he had indeed dispatched the olive oil. A few months later, I met Bush once again at a NATO convention and he repeated his complaint that still… no oil! Thankfully, the mystery was solved a while later: The renowned FDA –the US Food and Drug Administration– would not allow the olive oil into the White House because it was labeled 'Virgin Olive Oil', a category that the FDA experts had still not approved as edible! We attempted to explain to them in every possible way that it was intended for personal use by

• There may be only six grandchildren here but the picture was probably prophetic: a bus would indeed be needed to accommodate the total number of grandchildren to come.

• Grandmother Stavroula, mother of Kostas Mitsotakis, is seen here preparing her legendary "kaltsounia", following a traditional Cretan recipe.

Bush who was actually very eager to have it, but they would hear none of it! In the end a solution was found: We used a new label that read 'For external use only' and the olive oil got the green light for the White House!"

### Helmut Kohl's not-so-secret ice-cream visit

The former chancellor of Germany was also invited to stay at the house of the Mitsotakis family in Akrotiri, on May 1991, at the occasion of the 50th anniversary of the Battle of Crete.

"He was a cheerful man and well-known gourmet, who felt especially at home staying with us because he could converse in German with all family members," says Marika. "He was very impressed with Greek hospitality and kept saying to Kostas afterwards, 'I wish I were pampered like this back home…' But he had a sweet tooth as well! Actually, before visiting us that summer he had been to a health center in Austria where, after undergoing a strict diet, he had lost several kilos. After lunch, on his second day in Crete, he retired to his room to rest. Around 4:30 p.m., with afternoon heat at its blazingly hottest, we suddenly see Kohl going out of his room, crossing the garden and heading for the refrigerator shed where we kept the ice-cream for the children.

"Poor fellow, apparently he thought that no one would be looking as he slipped out to satisfy his craving!"

### Nutritious luggage for the trip to Nepal

The high demands of politics on one's private life allowed the Mitsotakises precious few opportunities to go on trips for pleasure, especially long ones. One such opportunity presented itself in 1993, when Mitsotakis lost at the national elections and the couple decided to take the children on a two-week trip to Nepal and India.

On the day of departure, Alexandra was understandably struck by the large quantity of suitcases assembled at the entrance hall.

"Why on earth are we taking so many clothes with us?" she asked.

"They are your mother's," replied her father who, however, did not further explain that the contents of the suitcases were edible.

"Cheese portions, cookies… oh, I had taken all sorts of supplies!" remembers Marika. "You see, after the 'Yugoslavia Syndrome' where we had gone hungry, I did not want to leave anything to chance, so I made sure we had all sorts of goodies available. Of course, the food there was wonderful and we did not get to eat any of the stuff I had packed. So before leaving Katmandu we left everything for the staff as a bonus, to the staff's utter delight. The funny thing is that the hotel's manager asked to see us in private and asked:

"'Is it true that you gave all these treats to the staff? They did not steal it?'

"He just could not believe it! Anyway, that was one amazing trip, truly unforgettable…"

### The prime-minister's "little sandwich"

It may sound funny for a man who systematically travelled abroad to meet with other prime ministers or to participate in summit meetings and yet it is true: Kostas Mitsotakis never left home without a home-made snack!

"Even today, the president takes a sandwich with him when he travels," says Emma, assistant-cook in the Mitsotakis household, using the honorary title of "President" conferred on Kostas Mitsotakis by the New Democracy party.

Katerina Mitsotaki remembers that often, when her father returned from trips and she would ask him if he wanted anything to eat, he would reply, "no thank you, your mother made me a sandwich for the trip and I still have it with me." In fact, because he hates throwing away food, he would often add: "There's a half sandwich left –would you like it perhaps?"

"Dad's were probably the world's most travelled sandwiches," says Katerina laughing.

### Passport-carrying food supplies

Another customary practice of the Mitsotakis family is the "export" of food as well as recipes to members temporarily residing abroad. Every one of its members has a story to tell about a suitcase that, instead of the usual contents like clothes, shoes, toiletries etc., carried delicacies to various places around the globe!

"In the end, I think my life has many similarities to the film *A Touch of Spice*," observes Kyriakos Mitsotakis. "There's love for food on the one hand and a mother's worry whether 'the child had enough to eat' on the other! When I

• The "tall one", as he has often been called, stoops to grandchild level for a friendly face-off.

was studying in America, every time I returned home for vacations the first thing she would ask me was: 'My boy, do you eat well over there?' Immediately after this she would ask me what sort of dish I wanted her to prepare for me and I would invariably answer: '"Dolmadakia" and *schnitzel*'.

"Often, home-made food would find a way to follow me as in the time when, during the period my father was prime minister, I was doing my basic military training in Tripoli. On the first weekend where visitors were allowed, all parents of the 80-odd recruits in my barracks came, save for mine and another fellow's. So I called home to complain and as a result, on the next visiting day my mother came bearing a huge pan filled with bite-sized, crunchy *schnitzel*. I started yelling at her 'You are embarrassing me, take them away!' but, of course, the *schnitzel* stayed and were devoured in zero time!

"Another time, when I was in London, a friend and I decided to throw a

• When surrounded by her grandchildren, Marika is always all smiles.

party. Arranging for drinks and music was easy but when the question of food arose, we had to ask for... reinforcements from Athens. They arrived almost immediately by air, in the form of dozens of 'dolmadakia' neatly arranged in multiple layers in a huge plastic container! Actually they tasted so good that we decided there was no way we were going to offer them to our guests... So we let the guests go without and we enjoyed 'dolmadakia' for a month!"

"In the early 1970's I was in Munich with Pavlos [Bakoyannis], where he was in self-exile," adds Dora Bakoyanni. "I was a university student at the time and I had only recently introduced him to my parents. So one day I called my mother to say that Pavlos wanted to invite to dinner about fifteen friends and acquaintances –exiles like him, and added: "I do need your help with the food!" In those days I was a total ignoramus when it came to cooking –I could barely manage to boil an egg properly! So on the eve of the evening party, a suitcase filled with 22 kilos of food arrives by plane from Athens! I remember the number of kilos exactly because they exceeded the airline's free weight allowance and we had to pay overweight charges! The suitcase's contents left nothing to be desired: lemon-flavored beef pot roast, 'dolmadakia', Cretan cheese, 'taramosalata', spinach pie and also lobsters that came with instructions for lobster salad. When he saw me claiming the colossal suitcase, the German customs officer sternly asked me to open it –he obviously thought that I was as suspicious as the suitcase, as I had my hair way too long back then. He almost had a heart attack when he saw the contents...

"'What on earth is all this?' he exclaimed. 'You cannot take any of it with you!'

"There was nothing else for me to do but to make a sacrifice of sorts!

"'Open the containers and taste it yourself!' I replied.

"Naturally, this would never be allowed today but back in those days it seemed almost reasonable. So the customs officer started tasting this and that –and he absolutely loved everything but most of all the 'dolmadakia'. He was so impressed by the food that I felt obliged to invite him to dinner as well!"

"The whole family came to Paris for the christening of my son, Yannis," says Alexandra Mitsotaki. "My mother, of course, arrived carrying the usual array of goodies for the occasion: ground beef patties, 'dolmadakia', spinach pie and so on! I had arranged for a normal cocktail buffet which was to be supplemented with Greek delicacies. I had not counted on the French maître who got so enamored with the beef patties that he hid them in the kitchen to keep them for himself! He finally... released them when we gave him the recipe!"

It also seems that the "cooking-by-telephone" habit is contagious.

"When he was thirteen, my son Kostis was enrolled in summer school in the United States," Katerina Mitsotaki says, "and he called me one day to tell me that, as an assignment, the students would have to cook a typical dish of their native country. So he called me and informed that he was planning to cook 'yemista', or stuffed vegetables.

"Are you serious?" I asked him then. "Why not an omelet or at least something simpler?"

"But he insisted and so, in the end, he placed a collect call to me –which lasted an hour– and I gave him step-by-step instructions on how to prepare them. This continues even today –he is living abroad and calls me every now and then and asks me to dictate this or that recipe to him, even though some of my directions drive him crazy!"

"'Please don't tell me «as much flour as the dough will take» because I do not understand what that means! «A little oil» is no good either and that also goes for «a small coffee-cupful of rice» because we do not have small coffee cups here!'"

The truth of the matter is that Katerina Mitsotaki has inherited her mother's talent for cooking and as she herself will admit, exactly because she is a natural cook she cannot memorize recipes.

"I know that this will infuriate Kostis once again but, yes, the eye can be the best judge and guide when cooking!"

## Travel mementos

Top-tier statesmen like Kostas Mitsotakis inevitably spend almost half of their lives in airplanes. Together with his wife, celebrated home-made sandwich in hand and chiefly in the course of official functions, they have enjoyed the hospitality of peoples of cultures vastly different from ours. Marika Mitsotaki recounts some of these experiences:

"Once we went to Japan to attend the coronation of the new emperor. On the first evening there, at the official dinner, I realized to my dismay that all courses to be served were of Japanese dishes. I do not really like all those flavors, sushi etc. and I was finding it hard to eat what was on my plate. Directly across me sat a Belgian official and I suddenly realized that she was sending me desperate looks for the same reason! So I silently showed her how to slowly move the food around in her plate, pretending to eat.

"French cuisine is very good as opposed to the British, though in both countries official dinners are lavish affairs. I remember one official dinner at the Versailles Palace –the one where Bush asked to speak to Dora about the olive oil. The whole setting inside the huge hall was like a scene from a painting: the tablecloth, the porcelain dinner service, the candlesticks, all were exquisite and each one of us had our own personal server standing behind!

"Generally I love travelling and together with Kostas and the children we've made many private trips to Europe, North Africa, Asia, and other places. A city that I love very much is Constantinople. I remember once we were there on an official visit and we were sitting in the hotel's veranda, watching the ships sail the Bosporus. Many were carrying the Greek flag and their captains –who knew that there was a Greek delegation visiting the city– would make a point to sound the ship's horn. This, of course, was very moving…

"Regardless, the Turks are always extremely friendly and great hosts. Their seated dinners are sumptuous, they spare no expense. They start with their famed 'meze' appetizers, then there is a first course and then the main course which is complemented by delicious pies with leafy green or cheese fillings, placed at the center of the table. Their sweets are truly delightful and very hard to resist."

"Many years ago," says Kostas Mitsotakis, adding his own recollection, "we were visiting Portugal officially, I as minister of Foreign Affairs. The visit included an excursion to the countryside outside Lisbon, where we were seated at a local restaurant for lunch. I asked the head waiter what he recommended and he said 'salmon'. Did they have cod by any chance, I asked back, because it's one of my favorites. Indeed –and much to my luck– they had cod so I was the only one who ordered it while all the rest took salmon. The upshot was that shortly afterwards all the delegates suffered from terrible food poisoning –all except me, that is!"

### … including *faux pas*!

"When I was heading the ministry of Foreign Affairs and also during my time as prime minister," continues Kostas Mitsotakis, "Marika had organized the kitchen exceptionally well. She also had a very good cook at her service, a man who used to work for the National Bank of Greece. The two of them had the kitchen section operating faultlessly. We hosted wonderful luncheons and dinners, always taking into consideration any special preferences of our guests who were often very high-ranking officials. Mitterand, for instance, was crazy about fish and we always offered him that.

"But we also did have our share of blunders! The Ecumenical Patriarch once came to Crete and we invited him for lunch. We had arranged to have lobster for the first course and then baby goat with artichokes as the main dish. That morning a friend dropped in for coffee and at some point he said:

"'Kyria Marika, today is a fasting day'.

"'Oh come now,' she told him, because that day was not a major religious holiday, 'I'll have none of this fasting day nonsense!'

• Still wearing her apron, Marika poses for the camera with Kostas Mitsotakis. Soon after, the table will be set and the call to dinner will go out to family and friends.

"And yet the man was absolutely right and as soon as we double-checked about the fasting, we panicked... Luckily someone had brought in two large fish as a gift that same morning, so everyone in the kitchen went into overdrive, a new main course was prepared and the day was saved!"

## Family customs and home-made dogmas

"I have wonderful memories from my childhood years," says Kyriakos Mitsotakis, "and especially from our family travels. I think we were very well brought up, with good principles and a respect for boundaries. However, the family dogma of good manners, so to speak, would be summarily cast aside whenever our mother started worrying whether 'the child had eaten enough'. And that is why, though my sisters had been raised under stricter rules, I as the youngest was rather spoiled: I would get away with the most preposterous behavior at the table without the slightest reproof from my mother, as long as 'the child finished his lunch'!"

"Today our get-togethers around the table are still intense affairs and we often have highly-charged discussions which are won by whoever shouts the loudest. We also have our very own customs that we keep without exception: In periods of national elections, it is customary for everyone to write down his or her forecast for the outcome and afterwards, whoever predicted correctly has full gloating rights! If I had to describe our family life in a few words, I'd say it is a life of discussions around the dinner table. I've heard it told that my mother is the undisputable headmistress of the family table but this is only partially true. My father oversees everything: He is the one who invites the most people over, the one who will make sure everyone has enjoyed his or her meal and that everyone is happy. He cares a lot about everybody…"

Some other dogmas, though, are not that easy to disregard as they have to do with… calories!

"Our mother," explains Alexandra Mitsotaki smiling, "does not agree at all with the contemporary views regarding nutrition, healthy eating, dieting etc. and does not approve of anyone who does not eat fully and heartily! In fact our family table is often the stage of Homeric battles between two clearly delineated camps: the health-food supporters and those who will never pass up dessert! I remember something hilarious but very typical that happened a while ago and has to do with my son Petros: Some years ago Petros wanted to introduce his girl friend –a refined French young woman– to his grandparents. So dinner was arranged and my mother prepared the usual three course butter-rich meal, complete with creamy sauces, dessert and the rest. So we take our seats at the table and to my surprise I see the young lady voraciously taking first and second servings from the serving plates which strikes me as terribly odd, because by the looks of her, I half expected she would limit herself to a few forkfuls of salad… So afterwards, I asked my son:

"'How come she ate that much?'

"'Because she was starving –I simply forbade her to eat anything during the previous 24 hours!' he replied. 'I wanted her to make a really good impression to grandma!'"

"It's true that my efforts for healthier eating habits are road-blocked by my mother's utter contempt for them!" agrees Kyriakos Mitsotakis, laughing. "Every time I mention healthy eating to her, she makes a face that speaks volumes, not to mention the pregnant silence meeting my question, say, about the quantity of butter used for the meal we happen to be eating. I usually address this kind of question to Emma, who has been with us for years and is the loyal keeper of our paternal house's kitchen, but she just shrugs to signal her hopelessness. You see, I try to teach my children to eat healthily, but when they go to Crete for vacations, it's a lost

• Together always, for better or for worse, in sickness and in health…

• Late 1980s, once again in Crete for the Easter holidays: Marika and the President of the New Democracy party standing proudly beside the traditional spit roasted lamb.

cause! Of course, I do give them very strict orders but these are circumvented the minute they set foot on the island. There are many who believe that my father is also a supporter of healthy eating but if you ask me, they are deeply mistaken.In fact, he is a gourmet and he likes to eat good food whether it's healthy or not!"

### Failures and beliefs

"Marika is first and last a nurturing mother," says Dora Bakoyanni, "and the house becomes a home because she is in it. An example of what I mean is this: We were spending Easter in Chania and she was absent because she had had an operation recently. The three of us were there, namely Alexandra, Katerina and myself, grown women, married, with children and housewives, all of us –Katerina, especially, is an excellent homemaker– and together we prepared the holiday menu. Well, on that Easter when mother was away, nothing came out right: the lamb was burned, the 'kokoretsi' was a disaster, a total fiasco! Of course we explained it away citing the proverb 'Too many cooks spoil the broth' but I think mother was really amused by the fact that we had failed so miserably!"

Marika Mitsotaki's philosophy of life is that too much love never hurt anyone. It is through love that she managed to keep the family together in good times and bad, even when its stability was shaken to its foundations.

"When Pavlos was assassinated," says Dora Bakoyanni, "my children's lives changed irrevocably, turned upside down. But in Crete everything was stable, things remained unchanged, and this gave them the peace of mind and comfort they needed so much. For instance, we will sit for lunch at two o'clock no matter what. I remember that [Dora's present husband] Isidoros was very impressed by this. I would call him at 1:30 p.m. and tell him, 'Get your beach stuff and come back home because we are having lunch shortly'. Keeping habits, sitting together around the table –these are important matters. They foster the feeling of security and stability. This is what will give you strength to hold your own against the most difficult of circumstances. It has nothing to do with money or social status; it has to do with something much more substantial and precious…"

## Preferences and habits

Notwithstanding her philosophy of love, Marika Mitsotaki raised her children setting clear boundaries and principles, which in turn were passed on to the younger generations thus precluding any extreme or fanciful behavior. Considering the family's rich legacy in culinary matters, it would not have been improbable for some members to have preferences, perhaps even capricious demands, but this is simply not the case.

"Quite the opposite!" explains Marika Mitsotaki. "The children have learned to eat everything and have no

• Seated in the veranda that overlooks the bay of Souda, Grandma and Grandpa are photographed in the company of some of their grandchildren.

whimsical demands. They liked everything I cooked, even when I was trying out new recipes. When they were little, I was very strict with them because I did not want them to grow spoiled, but then they grew up and went their way and there was no reason for strict rules anymore. Kostas eats all kinds of food, especially those that are not my personal favorites: all conceivable kinds of leafy greens and vegetables, bean soup, lentil soup, pulses in general. As for myself, beans are closely related to memories of the German Occupation, so I've never eaten beans ever since. I will not touch chick peas and prefer lentils and fava beans. I was not a fan of fruit initially, but little by little I changed and now I'm fond of them. I also love fish, all kinds. Sometimes I ask Kostas:

"'What did you eat when you were a child?'

"'A soft-boiled egg, maybe' he answers, 'alone, with greens or rice, cooked with oil'.

"After all, back then we couldn't even imagine eating any other kind of food, let alone the delicacies available today."

For Kostas Mitsotakis the day starts with a plain and specific meal: breakfast always includes a spoonful of honey taken with a glass of cold water, then fruit juice made from one orange, one grapefruit and one lemon, a soup of rolled oats and, when in season, one fresh artichoke, cut in pieces and sprinkled with salt and lemon. He also drinks a cup of Greek coffee with no sugar, which he avoids.

"I try to eat regularly, often and in small doses, always at specific times and of course, to take a smaller meal at night," he says. "Even when I was prime minister with a very full schedule, I made it a point to lunch regularly at 2:30 p.m. and then to rest by taking a nap. When we were in exile, I used to joke that there are only two people who sleep at noon in Paris: Karamanlis and I.

"I eat everything and I like everything! But even if you do not like everything there are instances where you have no choice. I remember, for instance, when I was at the School for Reserve Officers in the island of Syros immediately before the war in the Albanian Front. A local variety of big-sized cabbage, the 'mapa', was cooked together with rice to make the famed 'maporizo' dish. Of course back in those days no one took the trouble to wash the cabbage well and, as a result, the 'maporizo' was full of big yellow caterpillars! At first, we would not eat it. Then when we got seriously hungry, we would pick out the caterpillars and enjoy the rest! That's life, one must be able to adapt…

"'Generally food in our island is of exceptional quality. I have a discerning palate and I don't care if some people call me eccentric just because I insist that all eggs, meat and poultry do not taste the same. Some animals are home-raised, others are reared in battery farms. For instance: A friend of mine who has a herd of goats in the island of Kyra Panagia –a small, largely uninhabited island of the Northern Sporades group– from time to time sends me goat meat which is truly unique. It's delicious, with a slightly salty taste, because the animals over there graze on wild greenery and drink sea water.

"In Crete we make delicious 'kaltsounia'", he notes, "as well as all kinds of pies, like meat pies or 'tourtes' as we call them, which are made from meat and 'myzithra' cheese. We also have wonderful cheese. I always make sure we buy our provisions from select sources: we buy honey chiefly from the gorge of Trypiti or from Samaria, cheese from Mitato, made from milk of sheep grazing only on fresh grass.

"In Western Crete, from the Psiloreitis range on down, the staple food is boiled meat with rice pilaf. The meat is boiled and the broth is used to prepare the pilaf. My mother used to make a very nice sauce for the boiled meat. On the eastern side of the island the meat is paired with pasta. Boiled meat is the best appetizer to accompany wine. Cretan roast meat is celebrated as well. For example, lamb is either boiled or oven-roasted with tomato and potatoes. It is said that committed good eaters will consume a whole lamb overnight!

"Regarding 'tsikoudia' I can drink some people under the table but food I cannot eat in large quantities. That's why they say that if you are the guest of honor at a feast you should bring along some strong eaters who will do honor to the feast!

"Another famous product that I really appreciate is Greek olive oil. I am a producer myself, I have olive trees, I make very good olive oil and it gives us great pleasure to present it to relatives and friends. I take great pride in this!"

# Today

Crete, in the summer of 2011. The house is agog with excitement as yet another celebration –the marriage of Alexandra's daughter– is due and everyone has come. Winter had been difficult for Marika Mitsotaki: A new health issue arose and kept her confined –though unendingly courageous and optimistic– in the hospital first and for almost four additional months in a rehabilitation center in the Athens suburb of Paiania. Kostas Mitsotakis had been her most frequent visitor, a discreet and constant guardian.

"Since the olden times,' he reminisced one evening, seated in an armchair beside her, "what I usually find myself missing is Parliament. I am the longest-serving MP since the inception of the Greek state!"

"He would return home only after sessions ended, even if they happened to last till daybreak," adds his wife. "I would get out of bed and would go into the kitchen –in my nightgown, barefoot– to warm up supper for him, because I knew he had not eaten anything. Then I would keep him company as he ate, because one should not dine alone…"

And she still holds to this practice,

*Photograph: Georgios Papadakis – PAPADAKISPRESS*

• September 2010, at the garden of the house in Glyfada: The family keeps growing…

not just for the main meals but invariably for the morning coffee as well:

"When the children left home," she said in her earlier interview, "I felt bad. I could not stand seeing all those empty bedrooms. Now, every morning after waking up, Kostas and I take our coffee together. I read the newspapers and I tell him the news while he is taking his bath. Throughout our married life, he has never left the house without us taking together our morning coffee. Sunday afternoons hold one of our little weekly pleasures: I usually have a good movie ready to see on video and we watch it from five to seven before the visits and the phone calls start. We have good fun together. If you ask me, life and health are everything. This is my credo. Because I believe that –as the Cretan saying goes– if my husband is king, then I am the queen.

Crete, in the summer of 2011. Health problems are a thing of the past. The kitchen, overlooking the calm waters of the bay of Souda, is again a very busy place. Firstly, because everyone is here –children, grandchildren and great-grandchildren– having come in from Greece or abroad. The reason is not just the standard summer rendezvous at Grandma's and Grandpa's house –for the pleasure of sitting around the table, in the words of Marika Mitsotaki– but

*Photograph*: Vassiliki Georgiou – Focus Art

• Here are the first five great-grandchildren of Kostas and Marika Mitsotaki. Everyone hopes that many more will follow.

another special occasion: another marriage to celebrate, to raise glasses and wish for the house to be always full of smiles and happiness. And then it will be the time to prepare and photograph some of the dishes featured in this book. The air is filled with the laughter of children, the clatter of plates and glasses as the table is set in the shade of the veranda, the smells and aromas emanating from big cooking pots– the family is together again.

*Marika Mitsotaki passed away peacefully on the 6th of May 2012*

# Thank you, Grandma

There is an armchair in the sitting room at the house in Crete, a deep, enveloping seat known as grandmother's armchair. She is the only one who uses it, taking up all available space as she sits on it comfortably, placing her hands majestically on the upholstered arms. We, the grandchildren, would sit around her on cushions on the floor, since the grownups usually occupied all the chairs –and we grew up learning to obey orders, to revolt, to speak quietly as there was no need for us to shout in order to be heard, to argue on Good Fridays (right on schedule, every year), to love and to hate politics, to wait for the call to dinner.

Everything revolves around food: For the grandchild returning from summer camp, it's: "You're all skin and bones, my darling, didn't they feed you at the camp? Let's cook a 'pastitsio' as well then." For the older one who is getting married, it's: "Kostas, we need to find some sheep." For those that get pregnant, it's: "I'll fix you some liver with a nice sauce." Love earned by way of the taste buds –that's how she wants it, that is her way.

Our grandmother is a standard reference point for our family and the interpreter of our grandfather's feelings ("what you did yesterday upset your grandfather very much"). Scolding for this and that is part of her daily routine; two days going by without any scolding from her and we all start wondering if something is wrong. She will argue and squabble endlessly over petty matters while she will choose to stay strangely silent over major decisions. She dresses in many colors and accessorizes with gusto but never in bad taste. She adores being complimented for the nth time that the meal was perfect and, just to be on the safe side, her great-grandchildren get an early training in compliment-giving as well.

We had been asking her to do this book for years. First of all, because we wanted it for ourselves. So that all the recipes of Grandma and Nonika would be together in one place, coming from another age as they are, so motherly in style, so different from those of today. But now that the book is finished, we realize that every photograph and every meal is for us a separate memory, a part of our daily routine, a companion for the important events in our lives. Sitting around the family table we sometimes comforted each other, other times we misunderstood each other, but funnily enough we never lost our appetite!

All these years this family has often been the object of publicity of one sort or another and Grandma is the one who kept us together by inviting us over for yet another family meal. Lunches or dinners would serve as excuses to patch up quarrels among two or three of us; little, personal news or historic national developments would be announced with the family sitting at the table. And if our grandfather is the man Kipling refers to in *If*, then certainly this is so because our grandmother allowed him to be. Because, at the end of the day, we all know –with the absolute certainty one has about certain matters even though they remain unsaid– that everything is done for him, that every table is set and every meal is cooked, in reality, for him only.

13+5

# recipes

● savory dishes

# MOUSSAKA

**Ingredients:**

2 kg mixed minced meat
   (beef and pork, 1 kg each)

1 kg potatoes

1 kg courgettes

1 kg aubergines

3 ½ cups plus a little more (900 ml)
   tomato juice

2 large onions, finely chopped

3 ½ tbsp (50 ml) cognac

salt, pepper

¾ cup (180 ml) oil

oil for frying

bread crumbs to sprinkle
   on the roasting dish

**For the béchamel sauce:**

150 g butter

2 ¾ cup (180 ml) oil

350 g flour

2 ½ milk

400 g parmesan and
   Emmental (Swiss) cheese, grated

5 egg yolks

grated nutmeg

salt, pepper

50 g butter to scatter
   on the béchamel

cheese for sprinkling

**Preparation method:**

Heat the oil in a deep pan, add the onions and let simmer until light golden in color, stirring from time to time. Add the minced meat and cook for a few minutes. Add the cognac, the tomato juice, salt and pepper and let cook for about half an hour.

Slice the aubergines into rounds and soak them in salted water for an hour to minimize the bitter flavor, taking care to change the water 2 or 3 times. Gently squeeze the aubergines to drain, wash in running water, place in a colander and let them drain until dry. Wash and slice the potatoes and courgettes in rounds. Fry the sliced aubergines, courgettes and potatoes, then place on tissue paper that will absorb any excess oil.

For the béchamel sauce: Melt the butter and oil in a saucepan, add the flour and stir with a wooden spoon. When the mixture has turned slightly pink, stir in slowly the milk (which must be cold), then the nutmeg, and add salt and pepper to taste. Keep stirring until the mixture thickens. Remove from the heat and slowly add the eggs and the cheese, stirring all the time.

*Tips:*
● The layers do not have to be of three different vegetables. You may prepare the *moussaka* with only two different vegetables or even just one. For the children (and for Kostas) I always used potatoes only for one part of the *moussaka* on one end of the baking dish.
● To make sure the béchamel is lump-free, remove the pan from the heat when first adding the milk, whisk until smooth, then return to the heat.
● Ideally, the vegetables should be fried on the previous day to ensure that any excess oil will be thoroughly drained off.

Sprinkle the baking dish with bread crumbs and line with a layer of potato rounds. Season with salt, add a layer of minced meat, sprinkle with grated cheese, then add a layer of béchamel sauce.

Continue by adding a layer of aubergine slices, a layer of minced meat, a sprinkling of cheese and a layer of béchamel.

Finally add a layer of courgette rounds, a layer of minced meat, a sprinkling of cheese and a layer of béchamel. Scatter small quantities of butter on the béchamel and sprinkle with a handful of cheese. Bake in a preheated oven at 200° C.

*Cooking time: 45 minutes*

# BIFTEKAKIA (Ground meat patties)

**Ingredients:**

½ kg minced pork meat

½ kg minced beef

1 large onion

1 egg

2 tbsp (30 ml) vinegar

2 tbsp (30 ml) lemon juice

1 tsp parsley, finely chopped

1 tsp oregano

⅖ cup (100 ml) soda water

⅖ cup (100 ml) olive oil

¼ loaf (90 g) of white bread
(use crumb only)

salt, pepper

50 g butter for frying

**For the sauce:**

2 tbsp (30 ml) red wine

juice of 1 lemon

salt, pepper

**Preparation method:**

Soak the bread, discard the crust and squeeze dry the crumb. Place the onion and soda water in a food processor and process to a pulp. Place all ingredients in a large bowl and knead until thoroughly blended.

Shape the meat mixture into small, oval-shaped patties. Melt the butter in a frying pan and fry the patties. Remove the last batch of patties from the pan, then add a little warm water to deglaze the pan by scraping off the deposits from the bottom and sides. Add the wine and lemon juice, season with salt and pepper and let the sauce come to the boil.

Spoon the sauce over the *biftekakia* and serve.

· · · · · · · ·

# PASTITSIO WITH PHYLLO

**Ingredients:**

2 packets readymade thin phyllo dough

1 kg mixed minced meat
   (beef and pork, ½ kg each)

2 cups, approximately (400-450 ml)
   tomato juice

1 large onion

½ cup (125 ml) oil

salt, pepper

1 tbsp (15 ml) cognac

70 g butter for the phyllo dough, melted

1 packet No 2 pasta
   (or any long, hollow pasta)

**For the béchamel sauce:**

150 g butter

⅔ (150 ml) olive oil

300 g flour

2 liters milk

4 egg yolks

salt, pepper

grated nutmeg

300 g parmesan and Emmental
   (Swiss) cheese, grated

**Preparation method:**

Prepare the minced meat and the béchamel sauce as described in the *moussaka* recipe.

Boil the pasta in salted water to which a little oil has been added. Drain the pasta and mix with the béchamel.

Place 8-9 phyllo sheets in a deep springform mold, buttering each sheet separately. Add in layers half the pasta, the cooked minced meat and the rest of the pasta.

Cut the remaining phyllo sheets in rounds about two inches larger than the diameter of the mold and cover the top pasta layer, pressing in the phyllo's edges all around the form. Score the top layer of the phyllo into portions and bake in an oven preheated to 200⁰ C.

*Cooking time: 45-60 minutes*

# TARAMOSALATA (Fish roe spread)

**Ingredients:**

250 g *tarama* (fish roe)

1 ½ loaf (525 g) of white country bread

1 cup (250 ml) olive oil

½ cup (125 ml) lemon juice

1 large onion

**Preparation method:**

In a large bowl soak the bread in water, squeeze to drain and discard the crust.

Process the onion in a food processor to finely cut, place it in a blender together with the *tarama* and blend well.

Add the bread to the blender mixture, then the lemon juice and finally the olive oil in small doses.

. . . . . . . .

# SOUTZOUKAKIA (Meatballs in tomato sauce)

## Ingredients:

1 kg mixed minced meat
   (beef and pork, ½ kg each)
1 large onion, finely chopped
   (or 2 medium-sized onions)
½ cup breadcrumbs
½ cup (125 ml) oil
salt, pepper
1 chicken bouillon cube
6-8 garlic cloves, crushed
oil for frying

## For the sauce:

3 cups (750 ml) tomato juice
1 onion, finely chopped
oil
2 bay leaves
salt, pepper

## Preparation method:

In a large bowl mix the minced meat with the all the other ingredients, including the chicken bouillon cube (dissolved in a tablespoonful of water). Blend and knead the ingredients very well, then shape them into small, elongated *soutzoukakia* about 6-7 centimeters long.

Heat the oil in a frying pan and fry the *soutzoukakia*.

In the meantime, prepare the sauce: Heat the oil in a pan, lightly fry the onion, add the tomato, salt and pepper to taste and the bay leaves.

Finally, add the *soutzoukakia* in the sauce and let simmer for approximately 45 minutes.

*Cooking time: approximately 1 hour*

# ROAST PORK WITH POTATOES

**Ingredients:**

½ suckling pig (about 4 kg)

2 tbsp mustard

salt, pepper

100 g butter

1 wine glass (100 ml) oil and vinegar
    to brush the skin

**For the potatoes:**

2 kg potatoes

2 water glasses and a little bit more
    (800 ml) orange juice

⅘ cup (200 ml) lemon juice

½ cup (125 ml) oil

2 chicken bouillon cubes

½ wine glass (50 ml) cognac

6 tbsp mustard

**Preparation method:**

Mix the mustard with a little butter, adding salt and pepper to taste. Brush the underside of the meat with the mustard mix. Do this several hours before roasting, to allow the meat to draw in the flavors. Pat the pork and the skin dry before placing it in the oven, then brush it with oil and vinegar.

To prepare the potatoes, dissolve the bouillon cubes in a little water and add 6 tbsp of mustard. Peel and cube the potatoes, spread them in the roasting pan and spoon over them the lemon juice, orange juice, oil, bouillon-mustard mix and, finally, the wine. Place the pork on top of the potatoes and roast in a preheated oven at 220° C for about 20-30 minutes, then reduce the heat to 180° C and cook for two more hours.

Towards the end, turn up the heat if necessary and brush the pork again with oil and vinegar to glaze the skin. Test the skin for sufficient crispness by tapping it with a fork.

*Cooking time: 3 hours*

**Tips:**
• The same recipe may be used to roast a pork meat roll or a chicken roll.
• Regarding the orange and lemon juices used for the potatoes, quantities may vary depending on the acidity of the lemons.

# VILLEROY WITH SPINACH PURÉE

**Ingredients:**

**For the villeroy:**

2 chicken breasts (about 650 g)

1 onion, cut in half (or quartered)

salt, pepper (salt to be added last)

oil for frying

**For the béchamel sauce:**

100 g butter

100 g flour

3 cups (750 ml) chicken broth

100 g Gouda and Emmental (Swiss)
    cheese, grated

salt, pepper

grated nutmeg

1 egg

**For the breading:**

5 eggs

salt, pepper

1 packet breadcrumbs

flour

**For the spinach purée:**

2 kg spinach

1 tsp salt

1 tsp bicarbonate of soda

100 g butter

4 tbsp corn flour

1 chicken bouillon cube

½ liter (500 ml) milk

salt, pepper

250 ml double cream

100 g parmesan cheese, grated

**Preparation method:**

Boil the chicken with the onion, taking care to remove the foamy scum that will rise up during the boiling process. Cut the chicken in portions as desired.

Prepare the béchamel sauce a day before: Melt the butter in a saucepan, then add the flour stirring with a wooden spoon. Add the chicken bouillon, salt and pepper to taste, the nutmeg and finally the egg and the cheeses, stirring the mix constantly. When the sauce is ready, leave to cool and refrigerate.

The following day, remove the chicken pieces and the béchamel sauce from the fridge. Using your hand, take enough quantity of the sauce (which has now thickened) to thoroughly coat one chicken piece at the time.

In a mixing bowl, whisk the eggs together with the salt and pepper.

Dip the chicken pieces in the beaten egg mixture, then the flour, once more in the egg mixture, then the breadcrumbs and fry over a low heat for a few minutes,

until they turn golden brown on all sides.

Prepare the purée: Remove the damaged leaves and the hard parts of the root and stalk from the spinach. Wash thoroughly under running water. In a deep pan boil the spinach in a generous amount of water to which salt and bicarbonate of soda have been added. Let the spinach drain well in a colander.

Melt the butter in a pan then add the corn flour, milk, chicken bouillon, salt and pepper to taste and stir well. Add the spinach, already puréed in the blender (alternately purée the spinach using a rotary vegetable shredder).

Let the spinach mixture in the pan arrive at the boil and then add the double cream, stirring well with a wooden spoon to thoroughly blend all ingredients.

When the spinach mixture has thickened and is sufficiently cooked, remove from the heat, add 50 g of parmesan cheese and stir in to blend.

Sprinkle the remaining 50 g of parmesan cheese over the spinach purée before serving.

. . . . . . . .

*Tips:*
• For parties: Boil the chicken, cut it in small pieces, mix with the béchamel and refrigerate. The following day, take small quantities of the chicken mix in your hand, form them into balls and bread them following the same procedure as for the larger pieces of chicken.
• The chicken is boiled with the onion in order minimize the smell of the chicken meat. To enrich the flavor of the food we may also add a carrot, a few peppercorns, a leek, one tomato cut in four.

# BRAISED VEAL WITH AUBERGINE PURÉE
## (*Hünkar Begěndi*)

**Ingredients:**

**For the veal braise:**

1kg veal

1 large onion, finely chopped

3 cups (750 ml) tomato juice

½ cup (125 ml) olive oil

1 Greek coffee cup (60 ml) cognac

salt, pepper

**For the aubergine purée:**

2½ kg large aubergines (*flaskes* variety)

100 g butter

4 tbsp corn flour

1 chicken bouillon cube

½ liter (500 ml) milk

salt, pepper

**Preparation method:**

In a cooking pot, gently sauté the onion and the veal in the oil for a few minutes, then pour the cognac over the veal.

Add the tomato juice and 1 cup of water and let the veal cook until tender. Season with salt and pepper and let the veal cook some more.

To prepare the aubergine purée, roast the aubergines over coals or in the oven (under the grill), until their skin burns and becomes flaky.

Discard the burned skin and remove the seeds from the pulp of the aubergines. Place them in a colander and let them drain overnight.

To prepare the béchamel, melt the butter in a saucepan, add the corn flour stirring constantly. Add the milk, chicken bouillon, salt and pepper to taste and keep stirring until the mixture thickens –the béchamel is then ready.

Finely chop the aubergines, add the béchamel sauce and stir until thoroughly blended.

*Tips:*
* For the béchamel you can alternately use 50 ml olive oil and 50 ml butter.
* If the aubergines are not large, more than 2 ½ kg will be needed.

• • • • • • • •

# FRESH BEANS WITH SHRIMPS

**Ingredients:**

2 kg fresh beans (French beans)

1½ kg shrimps

2 tbsp (30 ml) vinegar

4 eggs, hard boiled, diced

10 pickled cucumbers

salt, pepper

1 tbsp (15 ml) Worcestershire sauce

1 tsp bicarbonate of soda

**For the mayonnaise:**

2 egg yolks

2 tbsp mustard

½ cup (125 ml) refined or corn oil

1 cup (250 ml) olive oil

1 tbsp (15 ml) lemon juice

1 tbsp (15 ml) vinegar

salt, pepper

½ cup ketchup

1 tbsp (15 ml) cognac

**Preparation method:**

To prepare the mayonnaise, process in the food processor the egg yolks, mustard, lemon juice, vinegar, salt and pepper to taste, then slowly add the refined oil and the olive oil until the mixture thickens. Finally, add the ketchup and cognac.

The previous day, wash the beans, top and tail them, then boil with a little salt and the bicarbonate of soda. Depending on the length of the beans, cut them in 2, 3 or 4 sections, then cut lengthwise in thin strips. Place the boiled beans in a colander, refrigerate and let them drain completely overnight.

The following day: Boil the shrimps with a little salt and the vinegar for 7 to 10 minutes. Then remove their shells.

Arrange the shrimps at even intervals on the bottom and sides of a round tube mold (save several shrimps for the fresh bean mix). Between the shrimps, arrange the slices from seven cucumbers in a fan-like shape (each cucumber sliced in three lengthwise).

Cut the saved shrimps in smaller pieces. Dice the remaining three pickled cucumbers. Place the fresh beans in a bowl and add the shrimps, diced eggs, cucumbers, Worcestershire sauce, salt and freshly ground pepper to taste and, finally, the mayonnaise. Blend thoroughly and fill the mold with this mixture.

Cover the mold with plastic wrap and refrigerate for 6-7 hours. Before serving, immerse the mold in hot water for a few seconds, cover with a serving dish, turn upside down and lift the mold gently.

*Tips:*
- If a mold is not available, mix together all the ingredients, place in a bowl and decorate the top with whole shrimps.
- For an official banquet, it is advisable to use the mold for a more impressive presentation.

• • • • • • • •

# KEFTEDES (Meatballs)

**Ingredients:**

1 kg mixed minced meat (beef and pork,
  ½ kg each)

1 large onion or 2 medium ones

⅖ cup (100 ml) soda water

salt, pepper

2 tbsp parsley, finely chopped

2 tbsp (30 ml) vinegar

2 tbsp (30 ml) lemon juice

½ cup (125 ml) oil

1 egg, whole

50 g breadcrumbs or ¼ (90g) bread loaf

refined oil or corn oil for frying

flour for frying

**Preparation method:**

Process the onion with the soda water in the blender. In a bowl, knead the minced meat with the rest of the ingredients. Using your hands, form little balls of the minced meat mixture, roll them on the flour so as to cover their whole surface and then deep fry them in a generous quantity of oil.

· · · · · · · ·

# POTATO PURÉE

**Ingredients:**

1 kg potatoes

½ liter (500 ml) milk

1 egg yolk

150 g butter

salt, pepper

grated nutmeg

**Preparation method:**

Peel the potatoes, cut them in pieces and boil.

Drain the potatoes and place immediately in a blender together with the butter, egg yolk, milk, and salt, pepper and nutmeg to taste.

Process mixture until thoroughly smooth.

· · · · · · · ·

*Tip:*
- If the purée is not to be consumed immediately, save a little milk to use when reheating the purée in the cooking pot.

# STUFFED TOMATOES WITH BÉCHAMEL TOPS

**Ingredients:**

1 kg mixed minced meat
   (beef and pork, ½ kg each)
12 ripe tomatoes
2 potatoes
50 g pine nuts
1 cup rice
2 chicken bouillon cubes
1 large onion, finely chopped
salt, pepper
½ cup (125 ml) oil

¼ cup (60 ml) cognac
a little butter or oil for the tomatoes

**For the béchamel tops:**

100 g butter
100 g flour
3 cups (750 ml) milk
2 egg yolks
salt, pepper
grated nutmeg
100 g parmesan and Emmental (Swiss)
   cheese, grated

**Preparation method:**

Wash the tomatoes, cut off the top parts and reserve the top slices. Using a spoon, scoop out the pulp from the tomatoes, place it in a blender and purée.

Heat the oil in a pan and gently sauté the onion. Add the minced meat, gently cook for a little while, then pour in the cognac. Add half the processed tomato pulp, one chicken bouillon, the rice, pine nuts, salt and pepper to taste and bring to the boil. Fill the tomatoes with the minced meat mixture. Put the tops back on the stuffed tomatoes, place in a baking pan together with the potatoes (cut in cubes), the remaining processed tomato pulp, the chicken bouillon cube dissolved in a little water and season with salt and pepper. To glaze the tomatoes, dab with little pieces of butter or drizzle with a little oil. Bake in a preheated oven at 200⁰ C.

For the béchamel, melt the butter in a saucepan and add the flour, stirring with a wooden spoon. Add the milk and nutmeg, then season with salt and pepper to taste. Remove the saucepan from the heat and add the egg yolks and the cheese, stirring all the time. Spoon the béchamel into a piping bag with a star nozzle. A quarter of an hour before the tomatoes are done, take out the baking dish from the oven, remove the tomato tops and form decorative béchamel tops with the piping bag.

*Cooking time: 1 ½ hours*

# ROAST BEEF WITH PASTA

**Ingredients:**

1 veal rump (about 2 kg)

1 packet long, hollow pasta (or bucatini)

2 large onions, finely chopped

½ cup (125 ml) olive oil

3 large carrots, diced

½ bunch Greek celery (leaf or cutting
    celery), finely chopped

4 cups (1000 ml) tomato juice

salt, pepper

¼ cup (60 ml) cognac

**Preparation method:**

Wash the meat very well and let it drain and dry.

Heat the oil in a cooking pot, add the meat and brown it on all sides. Add the onion and cook gently for a few minutes, then add the cognac and the tomato juice.

When the meat has started to turn tender, add the diced carrots, Greek celery, salt and pepper to taste and continue stewing until the carrots are done.

Serve the meat with thick pasta, cooked according to the instructions on the packet.

Strain the pasta, dab with butter and mix well.

· · · · · · · ·

# YOUVETSI (Braised meat and orzo casserole)

**Ingredients:**

1 kg of meat, cubed

1 large onion, finely cut

4 cups (1000 ml) tomato juice

½ cup (125 ml) oil

1 packet orzo (puntette) pasta

¼ cup (60 ml) cognac

grated cheese to sprinkle

3 water glasses (1050 ml) water

a little oil for the orzo (puntette) pasta

**For the meat marinade:**

2 water glasses (700 ml) red wine

1 onion, quartered

a few peppercorns

3 bay leaves

1 carrot

lemon rind of one lemon

*Let the meat marinate
in the fridge overnight.*

**Preparation method:**

Heat the oil in a cooking pot and brown the meat on all sides. Remove the meat, add the onion and gently sauté until tender. Return the meat to the pot, add the cognac and pour in half the marinade. Add the tomato juice and salt and pepper to taste. Cover and let cook at a light simmer for about 2 hours.

Preheat the oven to 200⁰ C. In a large earthenware dish (or baking pan or ovenproof glass dish) scatter the orzo (puntette), pour the 3 water glassfuls of hot water, a little salt, a little oil and a small quantity of the meat sauce –to give the stock a light pink color–, then stir to blend and let cook for 15 minutes. Please note that it may be necessary to add water at some point. When the pasta is half done, add the meat and –after reserving some sauce to use later– add the remaining meat sauce and stir. Towards the end of the cooking time, spoon the reserved sauce over the contents of the dish and sprinkle with the grated cheese.

*Cooking time: 25-30 minutes*

**Tip:**

• For the *youvetsi* you may use veal, lamb or goat meat. Since lamb or goat meat come with bone, a larger quantity of meat should be bought to compensate for the weight lost after deboning.

# STUFFED COURGETTES

**Ingredients:**

1 kg mixed minced meat
  (beef and pork, ½ kg each)
20 courgettes
1 large onion (or 2 medium onions)
  finely chopped
½ cup rice
salt, pepper
⅓ cup (80 ml) oil
2 tbsp parsley, finely chopped
1 chicken bouillon cube
1 chicken bouillon, dissolved in water
¼ cup (60 ml) tomato juice

50 g butter or oil
1 tsp tomato paste (optional)

**For the egg-lemon
–or *avgolemono*– sauce:**

3 egg yolks
juice of 1 or 2 lemons
3 cups (750 ml) broth from the
  courgettes (perhaps a little more)
1 chicken bouillon cube
2-3 tbsp corn flour
salt, pepper
2 tbsp (30 ml) evaporated milk

**Preparation method:**

Carefully clean the skin of the courgettes and wash well.

Slice off one end of the courgettes and scoop out their insides with the special tool. Place half of this quantity in the food processor and chop finely.

Heat the oil in a pan and lightly sauté the onion with the chicken bouillon cube. Add the chopped courgette insides and sauté for a few more minutes.

Remove the pan from the heat and pour its contents in a large mixing bowl, adding the minced meat, rice, parsley, salt and pepper to taste. Knead well to thoroughly blend the ingredients.

Spoon the filling into the courgettes and place them upright in a cooking pot. Pour in enough water to cover them then add the tomato juice, chicken bouillon cube and butter. Boil the courgettes in medium heat until the rice and the courgettes are done.

To prepare the *avgolemono* sauce, place the egg yolks and the lemon juice in a saucepan and whisk well. Add the broth from the courgettes and bring to the boil. Add the corn flour, chicken bouillon cube and season with salt and pepper. Cook until the sauce thickens and finally stir in the evaporated milk.

Spoon the *avgolemono* sauce over the courgettes and serve.

*Cooking time: approximately 1 hour*

# DOLMADAKIA (Stuffed vine leaves)

**Ingredients:**

1 kg mixed minced meat
  (beef and pork, ½ kg each)

3 tbsp parsley, finely chopped

2 large onions, finely chopped

broth from one free range chicken

1 cup (250 ml) olive oil

½ cup rice

salt, pepper

500 g fresh vine leaves

50 g butter or *staka*\*

**For the egg-lemon
– or *avgolemono* – sauce:**

3 egg yolks

2-3 tbsp lemon juice

3 tbsp corn flour

3 cups (750 ml) broth
  from the *dolmadakia*

1 chicken bouillon cube

salt, pepper

2 tbsp (30 ml) evaporated milk

**Preparation method:**

Wash the vine leaves and scald in boiling water for a few minutes. Drain and let them cool.

In a large bowl, place all the ingredients except the butter and the broth and knead well. Place a small quantity of the minced meat mixture in each vine leaf and wrap into elongated *dolmadakia*. Place the *dolmadakia* in the pot snugly next to one another, leaving no empty spots. Pour enough chicken broth to cover the *dolmadakia*. Add the butter or the *staka* and cover the *dolmadakia* with a plate (upside down) for the duration of the boil.

To prepare the *avgolemono* sauce, place the egg yolks and the lemon juice in a saucepan and blend well. Add the broth from the *dolmadakia* and let boil for a few minutes. Add the chicken bouillon cube, salt and pepper to taste, and the corn flour, stirring. Cook until the *avgolemono* thickens and finally, stir in the evaporated milk.

Spoon the *avgolemono* over the *dolmadakia* and serve.

The *dolmadakia* may be served with *staka* as a side dish together with the *avgolemono*.

*Cooking time: approximately 1 hour over low heat*

\* Staka *is a very tasty Cretan product collected from the cream of a mix of goat and sheep's milk. It is available at shops specializing in Cretan foodstuffs.*

**Tips:**
• Use any leftover vine leaves to cover the *dolmadakia* in the pot, then place the plate over them upside down.
• Buy the vine leaves when they are in season. Cut off their stalks, wash and clean well, scald with boiling water and let cool. Divide the vine leaves in portions of 500 g (weighted before scalding), place in bags and freeze.
• The broth from the boiled free range chicken will impart a wonderful, rich taste to the *dolmadakia*, but alternatively you may use broth from 1-2 chicken bouillon cubes.

# MEAT LOAF

**Ingredients:**

1 kg mixed minced meat
   (beef and pork, ½ kg each)
   for two loaves
4 eggs, hard boiled, shelled
2 onions, finely chopped
½ cup breadcrumbs
1 chicken bouillon cube,
   dissolved in a little water
salt, pepper
½ cup (125 ml) oil
1 egg white
1 cup breadcrumbs for breading
   and frying

**For the sauce:**

1 small onion, finely chopped
3 cups (750 ml) tomato juice
1 chicken bouillon cube
a little oil

**Preparation method:**

Blend together and knead all the ingredients except the eggs. Divide the mix in two.

Spread the two minced meat mixtures on a working surface and place two hard boiled eggs lengthwise on each. Wrap each minced meat mix around the eggs, making sure it is sufficiently thick all around.

Brush the loaves' surface with the egg white, roll them in the breadcrumbs and fry in the oil until they are lightly browned on all sides.

Heat the oil in a pan and lightly cook the onion. Add the tomato juice and the chicken bouillon cube. Place the meatloaves inside the pot with the sauce and cook shaking the pot every now and then (do not stir).

*Cooking time: 1 hour over a low heat*

# CHICKEN WITH RICE AND MILANAISE SAUCE
## (*Poulet au riz*)

**Ingredients:**

1 chicken

1 onion cut in half (or quartered)

**For the béchamel:**

100 g butter

3 tbsp corn flour

3 cups (750 ml) chicken stock

3 egg yolks

salt, pepper

**For the rice:**

2 cups rice

4 cups (1000 ml) chicken stock

50 g butter

**Preparation method:**

Boil the chicken together with the onion (skimming the foamy scum).

To prepare the béchamel sauce, melt the butter in a saucepan, add the corn flour and wait until it turns pink, at which point stir in slowly the chicken stock. Remove from the heat, stir in the egg yolks, season with salt and pepper and stir.

To prepare the rice, fill a casserole with the chicken stock, add the rice and butter and bring to the boil. Lower the heat and let simmer for about a quarter of an hour, until the rice is done.

To serve, line the bottom of a round tube mold with pieces of the chicken meat and cover with rice, filling the mold to the top. Turn the mold upside down on a serving dish and lift slowly. Spoon the béchamel sauce all over the rice and serve.

· · · · · · · ·

**Tips:**
• To impart richer taste and aromas to the food, peppercorns, carrots, a leek, one tomato and other vegetables may be added to the pot where the chicken is boiling together with the onion.
• Ginger may be added to the pot where the chicken is boiling to minimize the unpleasant smell.

# PARMESAN BISCUITS

**Ingredients:**

1 packet (250 g) butter,
    as is from the fridge
225 g parmesan cheese, grated
2 tsp (heaped) baking powder
freshly grated pepper
300-350 g flour
2 egg yolks

**Preparation method:**

In a large mixing bowl, cut the cold butter into small cubes, add the remaining ingredients (except the egg yolks) and knead thoroughly. Spread out the dough by hand into an even layer 5-8 millimeters thick and cut out the biscuits using a round cookie cutter.

Transfer the biscuits on a baking tray and glaze with the egg yolks. Bake in the oven at 200⁰ C, until golden brown.

*Cooking time: 15-20 minutes*

# KALTSOUNIA WITH CHEESE
## (Cheese-filled dumplings)

**Ingredients:**

**For the filling:**

½ kg *mizithra* cheese

½ kg *malaka* cheese

1 big egg (or 2 small ones)

½ tsp flour

salt

a little freshly grated pepper

a little spearmint (optional)

oil for frying (or egg and sesame seeds,
    if baked in the oven)

**For the phyllo dough:**

1 kg flour

pinch of salt

a few drops of lemon juice

½ wine glass (50 ml) olive oil

lukewarm water

**Preparation method:**

Grate the cheeses. Hang the *malaka* cheese in muslin cloth (*toulpani*) and let it drain well. Place all the filling ingredients in a mixing bowl and knead to blend thoroughly.

Pile the flour into a heap on a working surface; make a well in the center and place inside it the salt, lemon juice, oil and a little water and start mixing into a dough (in circular motions, gradually incorporating more and more of the flour). More water may be added –or not– judging by the feel of the dough. It should be firm but elastic enough to stretch.

Roll out the dough into phyllo and stamp out round pieces (using an inverted cup of tea). Spoon a small quantity of the filling –a little bigger than a walnut– on the center of each dough round. To close each round, lift one end, fold it over the filling to reach the other end and, using a fork, press the two layers of dough together so they will stick and close securely.

In a deep frying pan, heat a generous quantity of oil and deep fry the *kaltsounia*.

The *kaltsounia* may alternately be oven baked at 200° C, glazed with egg yolks and sprinkled with sesame seeds. In this case, the dough rounds should not be folded in half but in four.

* * * * * * * *

**Tip:**
• *Malaka* cheese is sold at stores specializing in Cretan products. If not available, the *kaltsounia* may be prepared with *mizithra* cheese only.

# HORTOKALTSOUNA (Spinach-filled dumplings)

**Ingredients:**

**For the filling:**

1 kg spinach

8-10 spring onions, finely chopped

1 chicken bouillon cube,
   dissolved in a little water

1 bunch dill, finely chopped

a little oil for sautéing and frying

2 handfuls of grated cheese
   (regato or parmesan)

a few drops of lemon juice (optional)

**Preparation method:**

Clear the spinach of all damaged leaves and remove the hard part of the stalk and root. Wash the spinach repeatedly under running water and cut (or shred) the leaves in large pieces as is usually done for salads, for example. Place the spinach in a cooking pot without adding water and let it wither slowly over low heat. Place in a colander and leave to drain completely.

Heat a small quantity of oil in a pan and lightly brown the spring onions. Add the spinach, the chicken bouillon cube and, optionally, a few drops of lemon juice. When the spinach is cooked, add the dill and the cheese and stir well.

Prepare the dough, then form and deep fry (or oven bake) the *kaltsounia* following the method described in previous pages for the cheese-filled *kaltsounia*.

· · · · · · · ·

*Tips:*
• The lemon drops, if added, will cause the spinach to darken in color, but they will enrich the taste and aroma of the filling. If lemon is not used, the spinach will retain its bright green color.
• Raw *kaltsounia* may be deep frozen to be cooked whenever needed.

# FRIED COD WITH SKORDALIA GARLIC SPREAD

**Ingredients:**

1 kg salt cod, cut in sections

oil for frying

**For the batter:**

1 can beer

2 water glasses (400 g) flour

30 g (2 tbsp) baking powder

salt, pepper

**For the** *skordalia* **(garlic spread):**

1 kg potatoes

1 head of garlic

1 cup (250 ml) olive oil

½ cup (125 ml) lemon juice

1 cup (250 ml) stock

    from the cod bones (or water)

**Preparation method:**

Soak the cod sections in water for three days to remove the salt, taking care to replace the water at least three times a day. Remove the skin and bones, boil and keep the stock which will be used for the *skordalia*.

To prepare the *skordalia*, boil the potatoes in their skin. Cream the garlic cloves in the food processor. Skin the potatoes and process together with the garlic to get a creamy purée. Add the lemon, the cod stock (or water) and, finally, the oil. Refrigerate the *skordalia*.

For the batter, place all ingredients in a mixing bowl and blend well.

Immerse the cod pieces in the batter and deep fry in oil.

• • • • • • •

*Tips:*

• If you intend to cook this dish more than once, to avoid the lengthy preparation before frying, you may buy a larger quantity than immediately needed and proceed to desalt, skin, bone and cut in sections all of it. Then, after reserving the quantity you need for immediate use, divide the rest in portions of 500 g or 1kg, place in plastic bags and deep freeze.

• For future use, do deep freeze the bones and the skin as well, because they will be needed for the preparation of the *skordalia*.

# BOILED FISH WITH SOUP, MAYONNAISE AND ATHENIAN SALAD

**Ingredients:**

2 ½ kg white grouper
    (or any other large fish)
1 kg courgettes
½ kg carrots
1 bunch parsley, chopped
6-8 small onions
½ kg potatoes
1 cup (250 ml) white wine
1 cup (250 ml) olive oil
salt

**For the soup:**

4 water glasses (1400 ml) fish stock
3 egg yolks
juice of 2 lemons
2 tsp corn flour
100 g kouskousé pasta or any pasta
    suitable for soups (quadrettini,
    seme di melone etc.), or rice
salt, pepper

**For the mayonnaise:**

2 egg yolks
2 tbsp (30 ml) mustard
1 tbsp (15 ml) lemon juice
1 tbsp (15 ml) vinegar
salt
½ cup (125 ml) refined oil or corn oil
1 cup (250 ml) olive oil

**For the Athenian salad:**

leftovers (fish and vegetables)
    from the boiled fish
salt and pepper (optional)
3 pickled cucumbers,
    finely diced (optional)
2-3 tbsp mayonnaise
    (or more, depending
    on the quantity of food leftovers)

**Preparation method:**

For the fish and soup: Boil all vegetables in salted water and when they are done, remove them from the pot with a slotted spoon. Add the fish, oil and wine in the vegetable stock and boil for about one hour until the fish is cooked. Remove the fish from the pot and place in a serving dish together with the vegetables. Save leftovers from the fish and the vegetables for the Athenian salad.

Pass the fish-and-vegetable stock through a fine sieve and return to the

cooking pot. Add the pasta and let boil for about 15 minutes.

In a small mixing bowl, whisk the egg yolks with the lemon juice and slowly pour into the fish-and-vegetable stock. Let boil for a while, then add the corn flour, season with salt and pepper to taste and let simmer a little until the soup thickens. It is then ready to serve.

To prepare the mayonnaise, place the egg yolks, mustard, lemon juice, vinegar and salt in a blender and process for 10-15 minutes. Slowly add the refined (or corn) oil, then the olive oil, stirring all the while –and the mayonnaise is ready.

For the Athenian salad, cut up in small pieces and place in a bowl any leftovers from the fish and any carrots, courgettes and potatoes not placed in the serving dish with the fish. Salt, pepper and 3 pickled cucumbers may be added, optionally. Add 2-3 tablespoonfuls of mayonnaise or more, mix well with all the other ingredients and refrigerate until serving time.

· · · · · · · ·

# STIFADO (Rabbit and onion casserole)

## Ingredients:

1 rabbit or hare

1 large onion

2-3 kg pearl or baby onions

½ Greek coffee cup (30 ml) cognac

½ cup (125 ml) oil

2 cups (500 ml) tomato juice

2-3 tbsp tomato paste

2 tbsp (30 ml) vinegar

1 tbsp sugar (perhaps a little more)

pinch allspice

1 bay leaf

a few peppercorns

salt, pepper

## For the marinade:

1 cup (250 ml) red wine

1 large onion, cut in two

3 bay leaves

1 tsp pepper, freshly grated

1 carrot, sliced

rind of 1orange (all of it)

4-5 allspice berries

3-4 cloves

## Preparation method:

Wash the meat well and cut in sections. Blend all the marinade ingredients in a large mixing bowl, add the meat and refrigerate all night to allow it to absorb all the aromas of the mixture.

The following day, let the meat drain in a colander and reserve the marinade.

In a large pot, heat the oil, brown the meat on all sides and remove. Retrieve the onion halves from the marinade, finely chop and return to the pot together with one finely chopped onion. Let the onions cook lightly for a few minutes, add the browned meat, the cognac and half a water glass (175 ml) of the marinade.

Bring the stew to the boil and let cook for a minute or two, then add the remaining ingredients: pepper, tomato juice, tomato paste, allspice berries, bay leaf, peppercorns, sugar and vinegar.

Heat a little olive oil in a frying pan and lightly brown the pearl onions. Remove the onions from the pan. Move the meat to one side of the pot and place the onions on the other side. Let the stew simmer over a very low heat for as long as it takes for the meat to become tender and the onions to be cooked.

**Tip:**

• Do not stir the stew after placing the onions in the pot. To move the sauce around the contents, gently tip the pot from side to side.

• • • • • • • •

# STUFFED TURKEY WITH POTATOES

**Ingredients:**

1 large turkey

*To brush and glaze the turkey:*

lemon, cognac, salt, pepper

100 g butter

1 chicken bouillon cube

**For the sauce:**

1 wine glass (100 ml) soy sauce

1 chicken bouillon cube

30 g corn flour

salt and pepper

**For the potatoes:**

3-4 kg potatoes

1 liter (1000 ml) refined oil or corn oil

150 g butter

1 cup (250 ml) lemon juice

2 chicken bouillon cubes

salt, pepper

**For the stuffing:**

1 kg minced pork meat

1 kg minced beef

1 lamb's offal
   (livers only, not the lungs)

2 large onions, finely chopped

1 cup (250 ml) olive oil

2 chicken bouillon cubes

3 green apples, pared and diced

1 cup (250 ml) tomato juice

100 g pine nuts

½ cup (125 ml) cognac

½ kg chestnuts, roasted

salt, pepper

**Preparation method:**

Prepare the stuffing and the turkey the day before.

For the stuffing: Heat the oil in a pan and brown the minced meat. Add the chopped onion, continue cooking gently for a few minutes until the onion softens then add the cognac. Cut the offal in small pieces and add to the pan, stir and let cook for a few minutes together with the meat.

Add the two chicken bouillon cubes, apples, pine nuts, tomato juice and chestnuts. Season with salt and pepper and let the stuffing cook.

Spoon the cooked stuffing inside the turkey cavity (reserve any excess stuff-

ing). Brush the turkey on the outside with a little lemon, cognac, salt, pepper, then smear with butter.

Dissolve one chicken bouillon cube in a glass of water and pour in a roasting pan. Place the turkey on it, dab with any butter left and bake at 200⁰ C. Remember to reserve the meat juices in the pan, after the baking is over.

When the turkey is done, remove it from the roasting pan and let it cool. Place the roasting pan on the stove and turn on one or more cook top hotplates (elements). Pour a little water in the pan and deglaze: using a fork, try to scrape off any remaining particles of the roasted turkey on the bottom and side of the pan. Pour the meat juices from the pan (including the scraped off particles) in a saucepan, add the chicken bouillon cube, soy sauce, salt, pepper and corn flour, bring to the boil and let the sauce cook for a few minutes.

To serve the turkey the following day: Empty the stuffing from the turkey (which has been allowed to cool) and place it in a pot, add the excess stuffing and a small quantity of the turkey sauce. Cut up the turkey in slices and portions.

Peel the potatoes and cut them into large cubes. Boil in salted water for 5 minutes. Remove from the heat and drain.

Meanwhile, preheat the oven to 200⁰ C. Place the oil, butter, lemon juice, chicken bouillon cubes in the roasting pan and place in the oven to warm them up a bit, then add the potatoes. Cook for about 1½ hour until they turn golden.

Place the turkey slices on metal serving dishes, cover with sheets of bakery paper, then wrap with aluminum foil. To heat the turkey before serving, place the metal serving dishes over pots with boiling water.

*Cooking time: 3-5 hours (depending on turkey size)*

**Tips:**
• A turkey over 10 kg will need 5 hours to cook. Make sure to check the roasting from time to time; when the turkey skin has turned golden brown, cover it with aluminum foil and let the roasting continue.
• Of course, the turkey may be roasted and served on the same day. Roasting it the day before facilitates slicing which is easier when the turkey has cooled down.

# MAGEIRITSA SOUP

**Ingredients:**

2 lamb offal (livers only, not the lungs)

½ kg sweetmeats

1 bunch spring onions, finely chopped

100 g butter or *staka*

100 g olive oil

4 cups (1000 ml or perhaps a little more)
chicken stock, preferably
   from a free-range chicken

⅖ cup long grain white rice

4 tbsp dill, chopped

2 tbsp corn flour

juice of 2 lemons

4 egg yolks

salt, pepper


**Preparation method:**

Boil the offal and sweetmeats in salted water for half an hour, drain, let cool, then dice finely.

In a frying pan, cook the spring onions lightly in butter and oil, then add the liver and sweetmeat cubes, stir and cook for a few minutes to allow them to pick up the onion's aroma.

Pour in the chicken stock, bring to the boil and let the sweetmeats and liver cook. When they are done, add the rice and let it boil for 10 minutes, stirring constantly to keep it from sticking.

In a bowl, whisk together the lemon juice, the egg yolks and the corn flour until thoroughly blended. Add a ladleful of the soup into the bowl whisking constantly, then pour the bowl's contents into the soup, stirring all the time.

Add the chopped dill and season with salt and pepper –the soup is ready to serve.

· · · · · · · ·

# LEMON-SCENTED POT ROAST WITH POTATO CHIPS

**Ingredients:**

1 kg meat

1 large onion

½ Greek coffee cup (30 ml) cognac

2 chicken bouillon cubes

juice of 2 lemons

salt, pepper

½ cup (125 ml) olive oil

50 g fresh butter

2 tbsp corn flour (optional)

potatoes

oil for frying

**Preparation method:**

Heat the butter and oil in a pan and brown the meat thoroughly on all sides. Chop the onion in the food processor, add to the pan, stir and pour in the cognac. Add the chicken bouillon cubes and fill the pan with enough water to cover the meat. Let the meat cook for one hour until tender.

When the meat is almost done, add the lemon juice and salt and pepper to taste. If preferred, the sauce may be thickened with the addition of corn flour.

Peel the potatoes then wash, thinly cut, pat dry and deep fry them in oil. When the potatoes begin to soften, remove them with a slotted spoon and set them on a dish lined with tissue paper to absorb the excess oil.

When the meat is ready, a little before serving return the potatoes to the frying pan and deep fry in hot oil until golden.

When done, remove the potato chips from the pan with a slotted spoon, season with salt and serve with the meat.

. . . . . . . .

*Tips:*

• All kinds of meat may be used for this recipe: veal rump, pork, chicken, goat, lamb etc.

• A very nice variation of this recipe is to use double cream and mushrooms instead of the lemon juice: After preparing the meat, heat a little oil in a saucepan and lightly cook a quantity of chopped onions, then add mushrooms and finally stir in the double cream. When the sauce thickens, stir in the sauce from the meat.

• Regarding the potatoes: The procedure described produces chips that are crunchy and very tasty, plus it saves time before serving, if the quantity to fry is rather large.

# SOLE, SHRIMP AND SPINACH CASSEROLE

**Ingredients:**

1 kg shrimps

1 tsp vinegar (for the water where
  the shrimps will be boiled)

1 kg sole fish

50 g butter for sautéing

50 g butter for the casserole

2 kg spinach

1 tsp baking soda

½ wine glass (50 ml) cognac

1 bunch spring onions

1 carrot

2 bay leaves

½ water glass (175 ml) olive oil

a little dill

salt, pepper

1 small onion

½ cup (125 ml) white wine

1 tsp coarsely ground pepper

**For the béchamel:**

100 g fresh butter

⅖ cup (100 ml) olive oil

250 g flour

6 cups (1500 ml) fish bone stock

salt, pepper

grated nutmeg

75 g parmesan cheese, grated

75 g Emmental (Swiss) cheese, grated

parmesan and Emmental cheese
  to sprinkle

**Preparation method:**

Boil the shrimps for five minutes in salted water to which 1 tsp of vinegar has been added. Remove from the heat and separate the shrimps' heads from the rest of the body. Reserve the heads.

Clean and bone the fish. In a large pot, boil the fish bones together with the shrimps' heads, onion, bay leaves, coarse pepper, wine, carrot and enough water to cover the contents. Boil for ½ hour.

Strain this liquid (fumet) through a colander. Pass the shrimps' heads through a rotary vegetable shredder, collect the resulting juice and add to the fumet.

Sauté the soles and the shrimps in the butter and add the cognac near the end for added aroma.

To prepare the béchamel, heat the butter and oil in a saucepan and stir in the flour using a wooden spoon or spatula. Gradually add fumet (approximately 6 cups) until the sauce thickens. Add the nutmeg, salt, pepper and finally the cheeses.

*Tip:*
• If the sole and shrimp fumet is more than the 6 cups needed for the béchamel, deep freeze the excess quantity for future use.

To prepare the spinach: Remove damaged leaves and the hard part of the stalk and root, then wash repeatedly under running water. Place in a colander and leave to drain.

Boil the spinach in salted water, adding the baking soda to preserve its color. Drain and chop the spinach.

Heat the oil in a pan, lightly cook the onions then add the chopped spinach, stir and let cook for a little while.

Spread the spinach in an ovenproof baking dish then add the dill and a little bit of cheese. Continue with a layer of shrimp and sole fish, pour the béchamel sauce over the fish layer, sprinkle with the parmesan and Emmental cheeses and finish by scattering small quantities of butter all over the top.

Bake the casserole in an oven preheated to 200⁰ C.

*Cooking time: 40-45 minutes*

# PASTA WITH SHRIMPS AND LEEKS

**Ingredients:**

500 g shrimps

3-4 leeks

1 ½ water glass (525 ml) white wine

3 bay leaves

1 onion, chopped

1 carrot

salt, red and black pepper

a few peppercorns

1 tsp vinegar

80 g (approximately) butter for sautéing

½ wine glass (50 ml) cognac

250 ml double cream

1 packet linguini

    (or any other kind of pasta)

**Preparation method:**

Clean and wash the leeks. Cut off the tops and the ends of the leaves, retaining for use all of the white part as well as a generous section of the green part. Wash well to clean away the grit. First cut the leeks in sections of 2-3 centimeters then cut lengthwise in thick strips.

Boil the shrimps in salted water to which vinegar has been added. Remove the shells and separate the heads from the body. Reserve the shrimps' heads.

Boil the shrimps' heads together with the wine, bay leaves, onion, carrot and peppercorns for 20-25 minutes.

Sieve the contents of the pot; reserve the shrimps' heads and the liquid (fumet).

Pass the shrimps' heads through a rotary vegetable shredder, collect the resulting juice and add to the fumet.

Melt the butter in a large frying pan or skillet and lightly fry the leeks. Cover the pan to keep the leeks from turning dark. Add the shrimps, cognac and double cream and bring the sauce to the boil. When the sauce starts to thicken, season with salt and red and black pepper. Stir the pink fumet into the thickened sauce, taking care not to add too much as it would dilute the sauce.

Boil the linguini in salted water with a little oil then drain. In a serving dish, mix well with the leek sauce and serve.

• • • • • • •

*Tips:*

• The quantity of the leeks should be equal to if not greater than the quantity of the shrimps. For instance, if the shrimps fill half a bowl, then the leeks should fill more than half a bowl. Accordingly, if they fill a bowl completely, then the leeks should fill more than a full bowl.

• For any fumet left after the preparation of the sauce: If it is substantial in quantity, freeze it for future use. If the quantity is small, add it to the water where the linguini will be boiled.

# CRÊPES WITH SALMON FILLING

**Ingredients (for 14 crêpes):**

**For the crêpe batter:**

1 cup flour

1 cup (250 ml) milk

1 cup (250 ml) water

2 eggs

1 tsp baking powder

½ tsp salt

butter for frying

50 g butter to dot the crêpes

**For the filling:**

smoked salmon (depending
   on the size of the slices, allow one
   slice or half a slice for each crêpe)

600 g cream cheese

a little chopped dill

1 carton (250 ml) double cream

½ cup (125 ml) white wine

½ cup (125 ml) lemon juice

freshly grated pepper

a small quantity of Gouda cheese

**Preparation method:**

Prepare the crêpe batter. In a frying pan, melt the butter and make 14 crêpes.

Using a fork, mix the cream cheese with as much fresh cream as necessary to soften it; add the wine, lemon, dill and pepper and mix well. At this point, taste the mixture and add more lemon or dill if considered necessary.

Place one slice (or half a slice, depending on the size) of salmon on a crêpe. The salmon must not cover the crêpe completely; it should reach up to about 2 cm from the edge.

*Cooking time: 20-25 minutes*

On the centre of the crêpe spoon 2 tbsp of the filling and add a little Gouda cheese. Wrap the crêpe around the filling, pressing gently, then place it –flap side down– on a baking dish (or ovenproof glass dish).

Do this for all crêpes, arranging them side by side on the dish. Sprinkle with the remaining Gouda cheese and drizzle with fresh cream –just enough to moisten the crêpes. Dot the crêpes with butter and bake in an oven preheated to 180° C.

*Tip:*
• A very tasty variation of the filling is to blend the shrimps and sole fish mixture with béchamel sauce, as prepared in the recipe for SOLE, SHRIMPS AND SPINACH CASSEROLE.

# CHICKEN WITH OKRA

**Ingredients:**

1 chicken, cut up in serving pieces

2 kg okra

salt, pepper

3 cups (750 ml) tomato juice

⅖ cup (100 ml) cognac

1 onion, finely chopped

oil for frying

some vinegar to drizzle the okra

**Preparation method:**

Trim the tough stems of the okra. Wash well and spread on a large metal tray. Salt and drizzle with vinegar.

Let the okra out in the sun for about an hour until they wither, place in a colander, wash under running water and let drain.

Wash the chicken portions very well then pat dry. Heat the oil in a pan and brown the chicken portions on all sides.

*Cooking time: approximately 1 hour*

Fry the okra in another pan.

Heat some oil in a cooking pot, add the chicken portions and the onion and let fry gently for a few minutes. Pour in the cognac, then the tomato juice. Add some water if necessary.

When the chicken meat is almost done, add the pre-fried okra to the pot. Season with salt and pepper at the end of the cooking time.

*Tips:*
• If using frozen okra: Wash away the ice, pat dry, then fry.
• For a lighter dish, do not pre-fry the okra.
• After placing the okra in the pot, do not stir or the pods will break. If stirring becomes necessary, carefully tip the pot from side to side.

# NOTES & TIPS

1. Parmesan and Emmental cheeses specified in the recipes are basically suggestions for one salty and one sweet cheese that melts forming long ribbons. These may be substituted with other kinds of cheese, for instance Gouda, Regato, gruyere, Greek *kaseri* etc. Generally, any leftover cheese that is beginning to dry out in the fridge may be grated and frozen for future use.

2. In dishes with tomato sauce, always use concentrated tomato juice or, if available, grated fresh tomatoes. Always add a little sugar to counterbalance the acidic taste of tomatoes, if these are not ripe enough.

3. Whenever a recipe specifies egg yolks only, do not discard the egg whites. These may be saved in a glass container in the fridge for up to one week and used for cakes, pies and omelets together with 1-2 whole eggs.

4. Leftover stock from chicken or veal may be frozen for future use. It will enhance the taste of many savory dishes.

5. The quantities of ingredients specified in the recipes correspond to the family's tastes and cooking methods. Naturally, they can be adapted to individual preferences.

# recipes

• sweets

# BABAS AU RHUM

**Ingredients:**

21 g yeast

90 g butter, softened
   at room temperature

330 g all-purpose flour

1tbsp sugar

½ water glass (175 ml) milk

5 eggs, whole

**For the syrup:**

600 g sugar

3 water glasses (1,050 ml) water

½ wine glass (50 ml) lemon liqueur

1 wine glass (100 ml) rum

**To decorate:**

Chantilly (whipped) cream

pineapple rounds

cherries

**Preparation method:**

In a saucepan, warm the milk, dissolve the yeast and add 3 tbsp flour. Blend well and let the mixture stand for 10 minutes to allow it to rise a little, then add all the remaining ingredients.

Whisk all ingredients –including the softened butter– in the food processor for about 15 minutes and let the dough rest and rise. Move the dough to the *Babas* mold and let it rise all the way to the top.

Bake the *Babas* in an oven preheated to 200⁰ C for 20-25 minutes.

Boil the sugar with the water for a few minutes to make the syrup.

Let the syrup cool completely then add the liqueur and rum.

Pour the cool syrup all over the *Babas* as soon as it comes out of the oven.

Decorate with whipped cream, pineapple rounds and cherries.

• • • • • • • •

# 10 MINUTES

**Ingredients:**

250 g chocolate (bar)

250 g flour

200 g sugar

250 g butter

8 eggs, yolks and whites separated

4 single doses of vanilla crystals
   (or extract)

salt

**Preparation method:**

In a saucepan, place the butter, chocolate (broken into small pieces) and the sugar and allow to melt over a low heat.

Allow the chocolate mixture to cool a little; add the egg yolks one by one stirring all the time.

Whisk the egg whites in the electric beater until they stiffen and form soft peaks.

Move the chocolate mixture to a large mixing bowl, add the remaining flour and the vanilla and blend. Next, gently blend in the stiffened egg whites.

Butter a round tube mold, pour in the batter and bake in the oven at 200⁰ C.

*Baking time: 10 minutes*

# SPONGE CAKE LOG

**Ingredients:**

11 eggs, yolks and whites separated

½ packet (220 g) powdered sugar

1-2 single doses of vanilla crystals
  (or extract)

5 tbsp cocoa powder

1 tbsp flour

pinch of salt

**For the Chantilly (whipped) cream:**

1 liter double cream

½ packet (220 g) powdered sugar

3-4 single doses of vanilla crystals
  (or extract)

**For the chocolate topping:**

400 g chocolate (bar)

a little cognac

2 eggs, whole

2 egg yolks

**Preparation method:**

Sift the flour, cocoa powder and vanilla crystals. In a bowl, beat together the egg yolks and sugar until the mixture is light in color. Blend in the sifted flour, cocoa and vanilla. Whisk the egg whites with a pinch of salt until they form stiff peaks and gently blend by hand into the egg yolk mixture.

Line a square baking tin with bakery paper. Grease the paper and dust with a little flour. Pour the batter evenly in the tin and bake at 200-250° C for 20 minutes.

To make the Chantilly (whipped) cream: In a mixer, beat the double cream with the powdered sugar and the vanilla crystals until the mixture stiffens; do not over beat.

Melt the chocolate bars over a bain-marie. As the chocolate starts to cool, blend in the cognac and the egg yolks, stirring.

Gently blend in half the whipped cream into the chocolate mixture.

Place the sponge cake on a kitchen towel. Spoon over it a strip of vanilla whipped cream and a strip of chocolate cream (but save a quantity of both creams for decorating). With the help of the towel, roll the sponge cake and freeze for 20 minutes.

Before decorating, cut off the two ends of the sponge cake to even out the edges. With a spatula, evenly spread a layer of chocolate cream on the surface of the cake. Using a piping bag decorate by applying alternate rows of vanilla cream and chocolate cream.

• • • • • • • •

*Tip:*
• Always be extra careful when beating or whisking double cream. Stop beating as soon as it thickens, otherwise the whipped cream will turn into butter.

# VASSILOPITA (New Year's cake)

**Ingredients:**

*250* 500 g butter
*250* 500 g sugar
*250* 500 g flour
*4* 8 egg yolks
*5* 10 egg whites
*87.5* ½ water glass (175 ml) milk *yogurt*
*1½ +* 3 tsp baking powder
*1-2* zest and juice of 2-3 tangerines
(optional)
pinch of salt
*cognac*

**Preparation method:**

Take the butter out of the fridge and allow to soften at room temperature. Process the butter and sugar in an electric beater then slowly add the remaining ingredients.

Beat the egg whites with a little salt until they begin to form stiff peaks. Add them to the butter and egg batter using gentle, slow motions to blend evenly.

Pour the batter in a round baking tin with a diameter of 39 cm, and bake in the oven at 200⁰ C.

To check for doneness, use a knife to see if the cake shrinks away from the sides of the tin.

*add xxx sugar*

*Baking time: approximately 1½ hours*

*2022*

**Tips:**

• Because the *vassilopita* burns easily, it is advisable to keep it covered with aluminum foil during most of the baking time.

• The *vassilopita* cake is traditionally cut in the presence of family and friends on January 1st. Previously, the host or hostess will have inserted a coin (wrapped in foil or bakery paper) in the cake, usually from the underside so the coin's exact location will not be apparent. Finding the coin in one's *vassilopita* portion is considered a sign of happiness and good fortune to come and that is why the ritual of "the cutting of the pita" is always an eagerly anticipated event.